The complete no-nonsense, becoming a UK pr(

The 1-2-3 on property investing

By David Tarn

In perhaps the most obvious fashion I'd like to open with thanking each and every one of you for purchasing this book, I'm aware it sounds like the typical opening, but it is a genuine thank you that comes right from the bottom of my heart. It is with a firm appreciation of modern living that I can honestly say that I am truly humbled that you would take time out what is these days a busy life filled full of choice and endless options to read the following pages.

To date, this book is by far my most significant achievement in business; it means a great deal to my current and future mindset that I have been able to produce something as momentous as this. I now believe, no scrap that, I *now know* that this achievement will help me elevate my success to the next level over the coming years.

If I was to rewind the clock ten years, I would never have imagined that I'd be sat here writing my very own book. I know almost everyone says this, but not in a million years did I think this would be me.
Coming from a typical working-class background, in the north east of England struggling through school with dyslexia, behavioural problems and a carefree attitude towards education, I was labelled by most as

the student that would never amount to anything.

This label is something that stuck with me through my early working life, so believe me *absolutely* when I tell you that the journey to this point in my life so far has been a long and arduous uphill struggle. But it's one that I have enjoyed and now furthering this journey excites me immensely. it's what, (along with the cries of my newborn twin boys) gets me out of bed in the mornings. So, my genuine appreciation for purchasing this book is a one that is true and meaningful and perhaps comes from a deeper origin than that of an academic.

I'm confident that the following pages will prove to be a useful and valuable tool, one that will aid you on your journey and hopefully one that will help you to get *exactly* where it is you want to be in the not too distant future.

Along with thanking you all, I would also like to congratulate you. This is not me being conceited, however. The congratulations are on making a positive step towards securing your financial future.

I strongly believe that by using the information throughout this book wisely, adapting it to suit your own personal situation and referring back to it on a regular basis, every one of you has the potential to be as successful as you'd like to be within this wonderful industry.

The property game is a friendly, exciting, positive and profitable industry to be a part of, but it is, fundamentally a game and it should be treated like a game somewhat.

That's not to say it shouldn't be taken seriously, I mean come on, we've all played monopoly and who messes around with that?
But unlike monopoly, it is not life and death.
It can dominate your thoughts and subsequently your life, and that's completely fine, it will help you to succeed somewhat, but don't lose sight of what is really important, there is much more that defines success and freedom than wealth from bricks and mortar.

Omitting the above statement though it does need to be shown a great deal of respect and a higher level of commitment than that of a nine to five job.
If one is to really succeed in the industry, there is a certain level of focus and dedication that is required. This dedication is fundamental to the success achieved. However, given that it can and often will, if you want it too, lead to total financial security and a level of freedom that simply can't be achieved with any job, it does come with certain responsibilities and can at times be incredibly overwhelming, but believe me when I tell you this early on in the book, however, that it really is all worth it.
It is an exciting journey with many highs and lows but done right, the positives, especially the end results far outweigh any of the negatives.

Although property investing can lead to complete financial freedom and security, If it's not given the respect it deserves, it can have a somewhat more detrimental consequence.

In general though, it will make the majority of people who dip their toe in a credible sum of money. This can be in the form of a little boost of income or maybe a small retirement pot right the way through to replacing your current income and in some cases much further beyond.

What this book is, and what it is not

This book is a general guide and is designed to illustrate the industry and its workings on the whole. It's one that should help you to determine what's right for you as an individual and is derived from real-life examples and scenarios from my own personal journey.

It equates to over 12 years of experience in professional property investing and many years of those, managing other people's portfolios. It will give you lots of useful tips and should help you to understand the fundamentals of the industry deeper. It should give you the tools to be confident in your own approach and should leave you feeling satisfied with the level of information received, without diluting the main points with unnecessarily expanded content.

It is, on the whole, straight talking and to the point, and sometimes this is at the expense of courtesy in-order to aid continuation.

It is not, nor is it designed to be a step by step guide on how to attain extreme wealth as a property investor.

It is not filled with unnecessary information that distracts from the point of the book to convince you that the author is something he is not.

Although there are many chapters of the book that will relate, it is fundamentally for property investing and not aimed at buying and selling property or flipping as it's called within the industry.
It covers predominantly investing in single let properties; however, the fundamentals for flats, HMO's and other investment strategies are very similar.
The information given on single let properties is mostly transferable throughout, so it can be implemented universally across the board, in most cases.
The advice given throughout the book is precisely that and is not meant to be a definitive conclusion to any aspect within. All advice, especially that relating to legal, financial and risk should be well thought out by the reader, and further advice should be sought after, before taking any further action.

If it were up to me I would have got straight on with the first chapter, after all, I want to keep my promise and adhere to the NO NONSENSE title.

The feedback received from the publishers, however, was that I must write a suitable introduction, one that explains me as an individual, I am to tell the readers or listeners about myself, tell them 'who you are' she said.

Well, in modest terms, I am nobody. I am of course me individually, but I am you and all of us together collectively, what I mean here is that I'm no different to all of you in general, yet I'm very different in a small and unique way just like we all are.

My DNA is 99.9% the same as yours, all that makes me, you, Jenny from the block or Albert Einstein any different is that 0.1% or the genome as it is referred to in biology.

Trust me when I tell you that neither I or any other successful investor or trainer you come across is to be pedestalised, just because we have already achieved, or are well on our way to achieving what you now desire.

There's a good chance that given the laws of nature you couldn't have achieved what I have already due to your youthful age or place in time so far in this world, and if that's not the case then maybe you were just busy doing other things until now.

That's fine, it really doesn't matter what the reason is, you're reading this now, and that is what matters.

You are now, even if you don't know it, already on the way to becoming who and what you want.

You've made a conscious choice to educate yourself on a topic that interests you; your subconscious mind will be absorbing material like a sponge as you progress, the more you tread down this path, the more it will become a reality. If you want this to become your reality just visualise your future, dream about it and convince yourself daily that you can and will achieve it, and soon enough you will be well on your way.

The great **Robert G Allen** once said *'the future you see is the future you'll get'.*

I believe firmly in the overall concept of this statement as will others who have adopted this belief. The people who have taken this view or mindset are successful as a byproduct, and the sceptical unsuccessful people? Well, they are merely further evidence of the truth within this statement.

So back to the answer to my publisher's question, who am I?
Ok, here it goes. My name is David Tarn, I am, at the time of writing this, 37 years old.

I have been a professional property investor for a little over 12 years now. By the time I was 32 I was in the top 2% of residential property owners in the UK, I have a predominantly passive income that long ago well surpassed my previous yearly job' income.

I now have a multi-million-pound portfolio which is structured to include many *personal* properties which I hold in conjunction with my wife.

I have properties invested within two separate limited companies, one in which I am the sole director of and the other which I am a joint director of with my business partner and friend.

I have within my ever growing portfolio a multitude of single let properties within the avenues above, HMO's or houses of multiple occupation and Joint venture properties with some of my family, friends & colleagues. I also solely own and co-run an independent lettings and management agency 'Wise Owl Property'. We as a company manage the sourcing, renovation, tenancies, lettings and day to day running of our own and our client's properties.

I also co-own a successful property training and mentorship company 'Wise Owl Property Training' which provides on-going mentorships for investors as well as in-depth training on specific aspects of property investing, including an in-depth analysis of this very book.

I am of course, as of now an aspiring author. That's really all you need to know about me right now; I'm going to leave my whole journey, one which has been a turbulent mass of highs and lows for another day, or rather more accurately another book.

For now, let's get to the real point of this book and show you how to strategise, source, view, negotiate, buy, let and manage your very own property portfolio.

What you must realise from day one is that the authors of the books you read, the trainers of the courses you attend, and the success stories of the investors you hear or read about really mean nothing in comparison to your success.

These people, definitely myself included are no different to you in general, by the best part we all started off from the same point in life. We all started off perfect, untouched, without prejudice and capable of anything and everything. The only differences between us now and the limitless possibilities we had as a newborn are the positive and negative influences we've received through our lives thus far.

These influences good and bad are unwillingly thrust upon us during our childhood, adolescence and early adulthood.

They are the *can's* and *can not's*, the *must's* and *must not's*, the *do's* and *do not's* that we hear on a daily basis throughout our lives.

This unwanted social hereditary acts as a barrier which aids the prevention of our development. Only when you realise and fully accept that these thoughts are not your own thoughts and that they have been unwillingly thrust upon your subconscious by unreliable influences are you able to do something about it.

There are no real differences between myself and any of the friends within my social circle, regarding ability, intellect or general cognition but there is now, a significant difference in terms of wealth, self-development, growth, productivity and success, or at least in my definition of the above.

As I've just mentioned we all started off, some many years ago now, the same, the only reason I have achieved what I have so far within my life and others around me have not is simple;
it's that I wanted it more than they did.
I sought it out consciously and subconsciously; it was just higher on my list of values and in a nutshell, that's it.

There is nothing wrong in the way in which others around you progress, and there is no reason to believe that I have somehow surpassed anyone in any particular way regarding the overall definition of success, but in terms of desire. Well, that's not in question, that's something in which I've well-surpassed everyone.
 If you want it bad enough and you genuinely believe it can happen, it will, and you will achieve it.
Just remember, success is a journey and not a destination.

In summary, whether you're an aspiring entrepreneur or merely want a couple of investment properties to help with your retirement, this book will be a useful tool to help guide you, refer back to and educate you along the way. As mentioned, it is packed with many real-life scenarios, examples of my successes and is compiled from many years of obsessive observations and experiences, that's the good and the bad ones. Once again, I would like to thank you for choosing to purchase this book, and I would like to wish you the very best with your own version of success, whatever that may be.

The five laws of gold

1) Gold cometh gladly and in increasing quantity to any man who will put by not less than one-tenth of his earnings to create an estate for his future and that of his family.
2) Gold laboreth diligently and contentedly for the wise owner who finds for it profitable employment, multiplying even as the flocks of the field
3) Gold clingeth to the protection of the cautious owner who invests it under the advice of men wise in its handling
4) Gold slippeth away from the man who invests it in businesses or purposes with which he is not familiar, or which are not approved by those who are skilled in its keep.
5) Gold flees the man who would force it to impossible earnings or who followeth the alluring advice of tricksters and schemers or who trusts it to his own inexperience and romantic desires in investment

George S. Clason – The Richest Man in Babylon.

These five laws were carved into clay by the great wise man Arkad many thousands of years ago during the heights of the Babylonian empire and have changed very little in the time that has elapsed since their carving.

As you can see by studying the above laws, it's *just not* a viable route to financial freedom to simply put away a small portion of your annual salary each month as 'savings' for the future.

This theory of stability is even more relevant these days than it ever was due to the low-interest rates and the rate of inflation in the current climate.

The so-called security you think you have from any savings is devaluing year or year which is the exact opposite of an investment or a wealth strategy.

In the simplest form, an investment in property is an investment strategy that *adds* money to your initial pot yearly and should, providing you've done *due diligence* create a surplus of cash to invest further.

The 12-month consumer price inflation rate to March 2017 was 2.3% - *meaning* your £1 at the 1st April 2016 would be worth 97.75p at 31st March 2017.

As I write this book just three months on the rate has risen from 2.3 to 2.9 meaning every pound you have in the bank currently and assuming the rate does not take a dramatic U-turn will devalue to 97.1p.

Now, this rate doesn't seem like the end of the world when used against the pound in my example above, but when magnified and used against £100,000 coupled with the fact that this can happen on an annual basis, well, it soon adds up or rather takes away, significantly.

"Leaving excess money in the bank is a fool's game."

I know that statement sounds a little harsh, but it's the truth.

All the top investors that I know, along with the wealthiest and most successful people I know, all agree that having excess money in the bank is deemed stagnation.

By this I mean, when we have a measurable amount of capital in the bank that is not pre-appointed to an up and coming project or investment or for the use as a contingency, it means we are standing still.

This stagnation is fine, I am not judging, I sometimes do this myself as I take stock, but standing still is not any companies overall objective or goal.

I am quietly confident that interest rates won't stay as low as they are currently, forever.

However neither does inflation, they often rise hand in hand but not always relatively and the state that our governments have got this country into over the last 15 years is scary, who knows how we are going to alleviate the masses of debt we have or what is going to happen once we finally leave the EU.

What is evident for me is that if the government thinks you have any funds or savings they can stifle or use to alleviate their obligations they will at any given opportunity.

They have already started to do this within the property industry as I will explain in depth later.

Governments will always seek funds from those who have them, those who are comfortable that is. They see this as the best or easiest way to obtain extra taxes without going after the larger so-called tax dodgers. There is little point in going after the basic rate taxpayer as often the majority do not have surplus cash to give; they won't go after the mega-rich for political reasons, so they stick to the safe 'middle ground', you and I.

It really is an old-fashioned, uneducated or unprogressive view, that saving for your future is a method for wealth or even security in retirement.
It's something that is thrust upon you by the older generation who simply don't understand the laws of money, and it is something that should die off when the time comes in my opinion.

It always surprises me when people get their financial advice, especially in this day and age, from their parents.
The kinds of parents who have had to save their 'hard earned money' every year to go on holiday, the people who work all the hours that God sends to pay the finance on their new car.
Do you really intend on getting your financial advice from someone who is not financially secure nor never really has been?
It may sound insensitive but if it's taken nearly 50 years of religious saving in order to pay off the mortgage, buy a new Ford Focus and be

"comfortable" in retirement, then maybe the financial advice they give isn't perhaps worth a great deal.

We live in the age of information and technology; there are now means and ways of achieving even your wildest dreams.
Take a step back and observe the person who is giving you financial advice and ask yourself some critical questions.
"Is this where I am heading", "is this who I want to be in twenty years-time", "is this someone I think has sound advice", "would I like to emulate this person"?

Think of the laws of gold and only seek advice from people who are either ahead of you on your journey or are the people you want to replicate. This advice, sadly, and with a small exception is not your parents, friends or work colleagues.
If I were to offer only one small piece of advice and be done with this book, I would say the following.
Listen to everyone, take any relevant portions of their advice, implement in your own way what the successful people have done and never and I mean never pay your mortgage down to save for your future as a means of obtaining wealth or security. That money is far better off invested.
If you want wealth and crucially freedom, then use any spare capital you have, even if that capital is within your home and invest but invest wisely.

How? I hear you say; well I am glad you asked.

Deciding to invest your money in property is a very wise choice if you desire freedom, wealth & security.
It's one that will help your money work for you just like in the 3rd law of gold, rather than your savings devaluing on a yearly basis as in the example I gave you earlier.

There is a fundamental rule in wealth accumulation that your money should work for you rather than you working for your money.
Once you grasp this basic concept, you can really start to gain momentum in the development of your mindset and strategy.

The investment property you decide to purchase to aid this rule rather than saving a little of your wage each month should draw capital as cash flow each month. This capital will add extra income to your initial investment and depending on what type of mortgage you decide to opt for and what your future plans are, this cash flow can either be a great little bonus to your annual wage or a significant step towards securing your next property.

One would be safe in assuming that over the term of your mortgage the property will increase well in line and most likely well beyond the rate of inflation in terms of capital growth.
If you look back historically, which is always the best way of looking into the future, as time and time again the history books repeat

themselves in waves and cycles, you will see that on average property prices tend to double at the very least all within the usual term of a mortgage.

A mortgage term is usually 25 years, but historically, this exponential growth generally happens every 12-18 years.

Why property I hear you ask, well why indeed I say, but unfortunately for you, I can't really answer this one.

What I can say though, is that for me and many others alike, it has proven to be a very successful vessel in acquiring the wealth, freedom and security that we desired.

You see bricks and mortar, as well as land, is generally considered to be one of the safest places to invest your money; now obviously you have to use due diligence here, do a mass of research so not to invest poorly or instead not to go into the whole thing blindfolded, but most importantly, of course, you must always adhere to the five laws of gold.

At the youthful age of 24, property for me was the only option I could think of that was going to create any kind of wealth. I did not know of or understand stocks and shares, I had no academic background to propel me into a lucrative job or career, (thank god!!), and I had no knowledge or experience of starting, systemising and developing any sort of scalable business.

I had, however, at that time been running my own gas company for about two years. This job, (I call it a job because even though I was self-employed, I was still exchanging my time for money), enabled me to observe all the landlords to whom I served tirelessly become wealthy and, in some cases, extremely wealthy.

This was the fruitful time of the property boom you see.

Now watching all these investors, part-time and accidental landlords become wealthy, *undeservedly,* really did at the time get my back up, it was only many years later that I finally realised that every single one of them was a deserved recipient of their new-found wealth, something I will touch on later in the book.

Never the less though, at the time I was begrudging these people of the ease of their wealth and the fact that these people were getting extremely wealthy ahead of me, as I saw it, for no reason, without trying, just a recipient of good fortune or luck, was very difficult for me to swallow.

This envy, along with my burning desire for wealth and freedom is what started me on my path, a path that took way too long to get going.

" The distance is nothing; it's only the first step that is difficult."
Mme. Du Deffand.

I know, from the many books I've studied and from the inspirational quotes that I value, that I am not alone in fear of failure, but for me plucking up the courage to finally 'go for it' was incredibly hard, *by far* the hardest thing I've ever had to do.

The self-doubt, fear and overall panic took control in me every time I got near to the notion that I might spend the small amount of capital I had taken so long to acquire, I almost didn't make the next step. The ridiculous notion that I may lose the small amount of savings I had acquired seemed to be far greater than the possibility of long-term financial freedom or success, and I believe that this is one of the fundamental issues that we all need to get past if we are to progress to the next level.

Our minds are our grates asset but can initially be our hindrance in personal development; they are hard-wired to be cautious and to hesitate to protect us from risk, in a somewhat hunter-gatherer fashion.

Only when you begin to take control of your mind and to reconfigure this hard wiring are you able to eliminate these controlling feelings. The way we do this is through our education, what we believe to be true today may be different to what we believe once we're educated on the subject fully.

"Our soul calls us to ever greater circles, but the mind with its belief systems hems us in until a greater idea from a more universal mind is brought to our awareness and then the boundary of our mind unfolds to an ever-greater boundary and that without end ad infinitum"
Ralph Waldo Emerson.

Thankfully, today all those unnecessary feelings are a thing of the past, they are replaced instead with excitement, hope and confidence.

I honestly don't give buying a property much of a second thought now, in fact, I can't seem to buy enough, there simply aren't enough suitable properties around in my catchment area for me to keep going at the rate in which I desire and sometimes that does frustrate me a little.

I don't view buying property in the same way as I used to, I now just see it as a simple maths or paper exercise.

If the figures stack up and I like the area or rentability of the property, I buy it, and it is as simple as that.

I do sympathise with those of you who fear the very notion of spending what can be a sizable amount of money on what you deem as *a risk*, I really do. What I can say, along with writing this book to appease these fears, is that it really isn't the big deal you think it is. Call me detached or insensitive if you like, but this is a sentiment that has been well earned.

Its said that years could be knocked trying off achieve your goals by following the advice of other successful people, people who have implemented a strategy that has worked, so I urge you to implement change in your mindset towards the attachment of failure.

There are many ways you can achieve this; you can educate yourself through the powers of positive thinking or even auto-suggestion. Fundamentally you can read as much literature as possible, attend some property training courses so that you are surrounded by other like-minded people, maybe seek the guidance of a mentor who will help ease these fears.

Of course, I have the benefit of hindsight on my side, coupled with years of experience, so it is a somewhat comfortable statement for me to tell you that this is a simple task.

Back then, however, before I learned to strengthen the positive neurological pathways within my mind through the powers of auto-suggestion and by further educating myself on chosen subjects, I had countless sleepless nights over the properties that I purchased.

As it turned out a few years later, some of those sleepless nights were almost justified, you see I, probably down to my hesitance and procrastination, doubt and worry, wondered if I was buying at the wrong time or the wrong price or even in the wrong area.

I did indeed end up buying a good few of my properties, not as prices were steadily increasing like everyone around me but almost at the top of the property curve.

Not quite at the top but not that far off either.

If I was to read years later about the wrong time to buy property you better believe that this was going to be it.

You see that's the benefit of hindsight, you never really know at the time if what you are doing is going to pay off. However, lesson learned, and I am glad it happened. This all taught me a precious lesson, probably not the lesson you are all thinking though.

Proper research, due diligence right?, Wrong! I did that back then; I did enough research for all of us to last a lifetime.

"a 70% good decision is better than no decision at all."
Wael El Manzalawy.

I want something to resonate deep within your thoughts here; I need you to understand that no one has a crystal ball, even the very best researchers or economists in the world still view their makeshift crystal ball through a cloudy haze of fog.

I bought some of my property just before the peak of the boom and a few years later, heading into the crash, they were worth far less than I paid for them.

Now the point I want to resonate here is that IT-REALLY -DOESN'T- MATTER.

I had no intentions whatsoever of selling any of these properties, the rent received easily paid the mortgage payments, and since at that time my tenants were paying the value of the loan down year on year, it bore no real consequence to me, except on paper, no one would ever know.

The lesson here is that unless you buy just after a big market crash, you have no idea what the market is going to do, even in this instance markets can continue to fall steadily. If you're buying for a long-term investment, then let the history books bring comfort and solace to your decision.

You don't want to wait for the right time to invest as that time will almost certainly never arrive and the consequences of waiting for a time that never arrives far exceed the consequences of getting the timing a little off.

Timing isn't everything but getting started is.

If you could have started saving ten years before you did just imagine how much extra capital you would have to invest now.

If you need further convincing of this, do some research into the fundamental laws of compounding, Albert Einstein called it the 8th wonder of the world, and *surely* that guy can't be wrong!

"A journey of a thousand miles begins with a single step."
Lao Tze

Making that first step towards securing your financial future, making your retirement very comfortable, increasing your current cash flow or towards building your property empire is one of the hardest things you'll have to do. This is so hard because it takes a tangible form, it takes physical action, it takes more than just talk, more than thought, more than simple desire.

There are many people that I've come across over the years that seem talk a good game.

These people seem so believable in their intent at first, but years later I still hear the same recycled words being regurgitated time and time again, many of these words now often come in the form of an excuse or justification for their lack of action.

The thing they all fail to do is not to plan or to have the desire but to merely take action, to take that very first step.

Once you action this first step, you will realise how easy it was or is. The value it carries will become apparent, maybe not right away but when it does become clear, you'll hold it in such high regard that for me it's right up there with quality research and knowledge of finance.

Taking this simple but crucial step will ultimately propel you to the next step which in turn takes you to the next step and so on.

Just like a snowball gathering pace down a steep mountain until you finally have what you want or desire, whatever that may be for you individually, success, freedom, wealth accumulation, security in retirement *or even a large snowman!*

I suppose it is my place here since you've been so kind to put the time aside to read or listen to this book, to make you understand what that first step is or at least should entail.

Looking back over the years at my journey in a somewhat clouded fashion or looking through the window into my world from outside you will probably see the first step as buying that first property way back then, but that's not entirely accurate. The first step does not have to be or is not that definitive.

The first step can be going to see your accountant, your financial advisor, your mortgage broker, maybe to book a viewing on a property or even to create a business plan based on your initial capital or desired outcome, current position or basic strategy.

You could enlist on one of the many training courses offered to you through the various avenues, including one of our very own specially designed courses.

Your first step is not talking to a friend or family member down the pub about what you're going to do or want to do when the time is right. It's not looking on Rightmove for twenty minutes a couple of times a week at properties that simply do not fit the criteria that you haven't laid out yet, and it's definitely not series linking homes under the hammer.

Although I acknowledge that these avenues do hold some minuscule value in terms of a person eventually becoming who they perceive themselves to be, they are not tangible actions, they are still based around idyllic ideas of a possible outcome and are somewhat detached from the reality of progression.

As I've already mentioned, to this very day, that single step was by far the hardest thing I ever had to do but be reassured when I tell you that it was indeed worth it and nothing at all to be afraid of.
If only I had adapted my way of thinking earlier and not procrastinated for so many years I would have bought before the property boom, meaning I would have been able to reach the heights I desired within only a few short years and I can only imagine where I would be now.

I used to be an extremely cautious, and relatively prudent person when it came to expenditure, in fact, there are many out there that would still call me a tight-arse.
These assumptions about me do fall short, however. I am still prudent yes, but by no means tight, *I do* like value for money, and I am, to a degree cautions how I spend my money, but tight?, no, you can't call me that, I have spent almost all of my surplus cash on property over the last ten years.

If I had all that money back in my account now as a lump sum, it would be safe to say that I'd be rather wealthy, albeit I have only been able to

reinvest significantly due to the powers of compounding so in essence, not all the money would actually be mine, if you follow.
And if not it will all be explained later on in the book.

"Where can I get my capital from" I hear you ask. "It's all well and good you telling me to invest by spending my savings but what if I don't have any"?

Ok, this is a question I've been asked many times over the years. Many of us want to progress in life, we want to acquire wealth or build something for our future, but again action is where this falls short. How many of the people that have asked me over the years where they can get capital from actually started saving a percentage of their income when I told them to in order to get themselves started?
Yep, you guessed it, none of them.
The lure of a new car, extension, modern bathroom, fitted kitchen, Mexican all-inclusive break or an uncontrollable desire to ignore delayed gratification tipped the scales in the wrong direction.
So, *I am* going to assume now, that since you've gone to the effort to buy this book and I have not made you read or listen to it, that you already have a certain amount of capital in either cash in the bank or equity within your current home or share pot etc.
If that is not the case and you still want to walk this line, never fear, there are other means of getting a deposit for a property. Some of which will be discussed later on in the book so keep reading because

all is not lost, in fact, far from it, there is one of the best-kept secrets in the property industry that will be revealed to all those who want to become a property investor but have no capital surplus.

Perhaps the greatest sin most of you have is the desire to invest but the excuse of capital being the issue of prevention, however, I would bet that the majority of you are sat on an amount of capital tied up within your current mortgage, an amount that in most cases would aid at least one purchase entirely.

Let me tell you abruptly now *that this* is not an excuse; you have the money within your mortgage, it's just how you view this money and the attachment you hold with 'paying off your mortgage'.

Let me point out also, your home is not an asset but rather a liability.

The hugely successful American investor and author Robert Kiyosaki defines an asset as being something that puts money into your pocket, and a liability as being something that takes money out of your pocket.

Answer yourself this one question, what does your home do?

Ok, so that's dealt with in the most transparent form, I could continue for the next 3 or 4 pages on this only to arrive at the same point, but I believe in straight talking and arriving at the point without unnecessary dilution.

Now, think about how you could turn your biggest liability into an asset. Remortgage perhaps? Hey, I am not telling you what to do here, but rather giving you the underpinning tools to develop your own specific plan.

You'll find known quotes and inspirational comments throughout this book, I am incredibly fond of them, and I understand, respect and value their origin and true intent on educating the recipient.
These quotes came from some of the most successful and educated people that have ever graced this earth, philosophers, physicists, astronomers, world leaders and inspirational entrepreneurs. People we should all want to emulate for whatever reason, being that of business, personal or for any other purpose.
They came up with these expressions of wisdom using prolonged observation and real-life experience; they didn't pluck them from the air like you see these days hanging on cheap plaques in our kitchens.

Take any one of these quotes for yourself, read its message, absorb it and understand it. take time to think about what the author is saying. You see, once you understand the meaning behind the quote and truly analyse it for yourself, consider why they were written in the first instance and for what purpose they serve, you'll realise yourself that along with Google, every answer to every question is already in existence. Someone has experienced it, succeeded with it, failed with it and you better believe they've written about it, good or bad.

This brings me nicely to my next and final point before we get started with, Part-1 'getting started'.

If this next statement sounds a little harsh, detached or just merely rude, then please forgive me. It is not my intention anywhere in this book to offend or antagonise anyone, BUT, there really is no plausible excuse not to succeed. There are hundreds of reasons *why not* to try to succeed, but anyone of us can or can't do this. it is *all* in the mindset of the individual and how high this 'success' is on your list of values.

Gerald Ford said, *"if you think you can or you think you can't, your right."*
This is perhaps my favourite quote; it very simply sums it all up.
It demonstrates that success or failure is merely in the mind, the most powerful tool we all possess.
I understand that there are extremities to the rule and that some people have either had a huge help financially getting started, security from birth or are in such turmoil in their life that it would be a disastrous choice for them to focus on investment at this point.
Let's for the purpose of continuation, however, just assume that these people are not reading or listening to this book right now and if they are, don't let their situation prevent you from getting started.

The person sat next to you in the bar whose grandfather left him 20 properties in his will should not stop you from getting started. Good for him, talk with him, get his advice or opinions, use what you need, discard the rest and get going.

Moving from the industrial age into the technology age has brought a plethora of information along for the ride, there is now almost limitless access to an ever-growing field of knowledge available to every individual.

There is a mass of online advice or information through websites, case studies, books, training programs, blogs, YouTube videos, webinars, podcasts and distant learning to name just a few. This information is so freely available now that it can be accessed in a matter of seconds, you just need to take the time to find it, read it and use it to your advantage. This is just another form of leverage, something in which the entire property industry is built around.

In summary: before we get started, I would just like to reiterate the main point I am trying to demonstrate.

Your mind is your biggest asset and also your biggest hindrance but with a good alibi.

For years its absorbed the doubts of others that have been thrust upon you unwillingly, this inaccurate and detrimental information is swirling through your subconscious put there by unreliable, uneducated and inexperienced sources. These secondary implanted thoughts determine your actions on a daily basis; these thoughts are your biggest hurdle now.

The good news here, however, is that they can be overcome, they are just an illusion.

Believe me here when I tell you that for the best part they are not your own thoughts. It may feel like they are because you've now come to believe them for yourself, but they are the thoughts of peers, elders, poor teachers, parents, relatives, friends and foes alike.

Your task now is to conquer them, to overcome them by filling your subconscious with your own positive thoughts and beliefs, and soon enough these old ideas will disburse leaving you with clarity.

My apologies if it sounds like I'm repeating myself here, but I really could write a full book on the phycology of belief.

It is the most fundamental thing that you must overcome, once you master this there is no stopping you.

The problem here is, and I do not want to sound negative but, statistically, the majority of people reading this book will never overcome these doubts.

Please don't let that be you; let us together, prove the statisticians wrong.

"How do I do this" I hear you ask.

Well, just read back through this last section, as all the answer are within.

There is no excuse in the age of information technology. Fill your mind with the positive influence of the examples above, and soon enough they will flood your subconscious and drown the negative cant's that exist at present.

Remember your future is determined by your subconscious thoughts, and you can, despite what people say, adjust your subconscious, you just need to believe in yourself as I do.

Part 1 - Getting started
Chapter 1, Assessing the avenues available to source property

So to the book, the real reason you're here, not to listen to me pretend to be Sigmund Freud.

I do think it is imperative that you understand the mindset behind the process from a phycological perspective, but you're really here because you want to learn how to become a landlord, professional investor or property owner and not a practising psychiatrist.

I'm going to keep this section, or rather some of the subsections relatively short and to the point.

I have already touched on the importance of getting started regarding tangible action, and hopefully, that point has sunk in well.

I'm going to assume that because you've decided to keep on reading that you are intending on actioning these steps rather than simply talking about them. Maybe you already have, perhaps you already own a property or two, perhaps you've viewed a property or offered on a property or at least have that intention, and you now want some good reliable advice on how to be successful with your investment.

If that is you, or whatever stage you currently are, then well done for getting this far and be assured that within this book lies the experience of lessons learnt to help guide you to minimise the mistakes and maximise your potential.

You will find, within the following pages some of the key elements to my success and If you listen to them, implement them along with your own strategy and refer back to them on a regular basis as a reference then therein lies a platform for building your own version of success within the property industry.

***Just a quick disclaimer* before we start:** my methods are most likely different from John's methods down the street and Brains methods across the river, and completely different to Julia's methods over on the coast.

I can't give you the complete golden ticket to success nor can I guarantee that you'll be successful, after all, success *is* measured by the individual.

There are so many variables that will determine your version of success. At the very least your demographics, starting position, long-term goal and availability to implement your plan correctly.

What I can say, is that I have been very successful in implementing my strategy over the years and along with many other professional investors what I offer, or we all offer collectively is sound advice.

You should try to read as many books, blogs and articles as you can at first to help fill your mind with as many variable opinions, thoughts and methods as possible. This way you can make your mind up which one or combination of ones you want to pursue.

Dean Karnazes writes in his 'ultramarathon man – confessions of an all-night runner' "listen to everyone and follow no one", this is a great piece of advice and something I encourage. He's telling you to gather all the information possible from all the credible sources then make your own decisions based on that information, something in which I echo throughout all my mentorship programs and training courses.

There are other books on the market that offer different methods to mine. Some have more in-depth, specific tailoring of strategies or relate more to funding or industry 'secrets'. Some of these books will echo my methods and opinions, and others may contradict them. They are all for the best part subjective and relevant to the level of financial success that one is aiming to achieve.

I wanted to tailor this book as a complete guide aimed at a generalisation of the newer style investor or landlord.

I will, throughout the book try to keep things fairly general so that you can get from it what you as an individual will need and try to keep to the theme of the book, one being aimed at a complete no-nonsense guide for the aspiring investor.

I can only try not to get too hung up on certain mind-blowing, in-depth explanations of specific topics, however when you have a lot to say that can be a little tricky.

I will at the end of this book list some very useful 'must read' books that I have found very helpful over the years, some of which are not aimed specifically at property investing.

One thing I will say is that my methods in *buying* or *financing* deals may not necessarily directly relate to property based in London or some other affluent areas of the south-east, I do believe London is a book in itself. However, the following pages will aid on pretty much every other aspect of property investing no matter where you are based.

Unless you've been living in a cave for the past 15 years, I'm sure you'll already be aware of many of the avenues available to source property, little or no experience, a rough idea or an expert, we are all aware of Rightmove.

I will briefly discuss the main avenues available to source property giving my thoughts on each of the topics listed below and hopefully touch on a few things you may not have thought of.

1) The newspaper
2) The estate agent, their window, website and phone-line
3) The internet – sites like Rightmove, Zoopla, YOURMOVE, On the Market and Prime Location
4) Property auctions
5) Professional property sourcing companies
6) Facebook
7) Friends, family, work colleagues or clients
8) Landlords associations
9) Leaflet distribution
10) For sale boards

1) The newspaper

Not much to be said about this one, depending on your age you'll still take note of it and perhaps browse through it on a Sunday afternoon. If you're from the younger generation, however, you'll not even be aware that agents advertise property in newspapers.

To be perfectly honest, I can't believe they still do, but that disgruntled judgemental observation is for a different day.

I have bought only one of my many properties through the medium of paper advertising, and even in that instance, I would have found it the next day or so online.

I don't hold any value to newspaper advertising what so ever and I can honestly say I never pick it up anymore.

I am quietly confident that it will be a thing of the past in all, but a few years. The way the world and in particular technology are progressing the future is not in paper and ink but instead in technology.

I would estimate that there is more than a good chance, perhaps up to a 90% chance that you are listening to this book or reading it on a digital device rather than reading it in its paperback version.

I listen to about five or six books a month but before I discovered Audiobooks, which I will reluctantly admit was after everyone else I read about four or five paperbacks a year.

I happen to know that the estate agents will all rejoice when they can finally stop advertising through the local papers, it is a massive overhead and a drain on their resources, and they simply don't need it anymore.

If they just got their heads together and agreed like gentlemen not to advertise in the papers, then they would all be better off financially and be able to increase productivity.

I used to own and run a local weekly newspaper, and the only reason one agent advertised with us was that their closest competitor did and so the vicious circle was complete. Great for us but not for their business. Apologies if you're in the newspaper industry, I do not wish you to be out of a job, but instead, I am making an obvious observation about how I see the future. The reason I mention the newspaper here is that in some instances local agents are required to advertise repossession offers for 7 days once they have been accepted by the finance company, just be aware of that. That's all I have to say about the newspaper, in my opinion, it's a cup of tea, and biscuit read while your gran is talking to you on a Sunday afternoon about the state of the coach toilets on her recent trip to Bognor. It is a medium for sourcing but a very unproductive one. It composts well though, so not all bad!

2) The good old estate agent

Like them or loathe them they are integral to your plans. Although I don't think the role of the estate agent has evolved enough in recent years and believe their approach does need a bit of a revamp. *This is something which I'm sure they will all agree on, and echo since the revamp I talk about hinges on increasing the profitability of their business.* This would be done by removing overheads such as the aforementioned newspaper advertising, their high street presence which they did once need, but not these days and even to a lesser degree, and I know this one may create debate but the amount of advertising or marketing they once did.

I understand they still need their presence to be in the public domain for the vendor's appeasement and I acknowledge that evidently that's who they work for but for the best part and heading into the future it is us, the investors who really keep things flowing.

Their now mandatory online platform through sites like Rightmove is by far their biggest asset, even surpassing their own online presence. In fact, in my opinion, it is the only tool they need to fundamentally maintain. Just look at companies like Purple Bricks popping up without local offices. Purple Bricks are the fastest growing estate agents in the country, and they have a completely different approach, one in which they don't see value in local offices. I believe we are heading into an

American style *real estate* way of doing things and I fully condone this progression.

Although I believe my opinions are valid, I do think the estate agents are one of the most valuable tools for locating property.
I was quite specific on my list above when I mentioned in point 2, 'The estate agent', their window, online presence and phone-line' the key element here is their phone line. If there is one thing that the technology age doesn't bring it's the one to one interaction we used to have. The personal touch and service that we all like is becoming a thing of the past but believe me when I tell you that this personal one to one communication and face to face interaction still has a massive part to play within this industry.
I advise every one of you to pick up the phone, introduce yourself, explain your position and intentions and ask their availability so that you can request a face to face discussion with their property manager. This way you can truly give them a firm understanding of what your needs and criteria are for property.

Forming personal relationships with agents is something that took me way too long to develop as I never understood or appreciated the benefit or its value.
I viewed agents as unreliable, false in their intent, lacking in respect and amongst all else poor-quality advisers. Now, some of this may sound harsh or even be true to some degree, as they can be difficult to

work with sometimes, however, I sit here editing this book currently completing on three properties that never even got to-let boards erected, one didn't even make it on to Rightmove.

This is because I have, over the years since realising their value, made my position and intent very clear to the selected few that I wish to work with on a regular basis.

They know my criteria for a property, they know my preference and immediate position, and sometimes they even surprise me with properties that are outside of this criterion, just like one of the properties above. This property was outside of my usual preference, but once I ran the numbers through my spreadsheet I found that it made more than good sense from a cash flow point of view to buy it, so I bought it, and I thank him dearly for bringing it to my attention. We now get phone calls or emails on a daily basis from agents who know our specific criteria clearly, and I don't mean the general property emails we used to get spammed with on a regular basis, I mean personal emails with very good potentially suitable properties.

I also receive personal text messages from some of the property managers in the local branches informing me of properties they've been to value over the past few days, this creates a significant advantage for me as a professional investor and is a mutually beneficial arrangement for us both collectively. I get to know about certain properties before they hit the mainstream and the agents get to tell the vendors that they may already have someone interested in their property, securing them the instruction to act and giving me a head start in the research department.

In summary, it is paramount to your business or investment strategy that you approach the agents and introduce yourself, just make sure they afford you the time of a face to face meeting. Agents that don't do this, I would question their intent and professionalism going forward. This is why we only work closely with a few agents in our area, although I still do buy from others from time to time, I am not into cutting my nose off to spite my face entirely.

One thing I will say is that you may need to be persistent here. Agents do get inundated with aspiring investors informing them of their intent, an intent that may not always be acted upon, once they realise that you are serious and in a position to proceed, however, they will see your value, and you will be their first port of call soon enough.

3) The internet – sites like Rightmove, Zoopla, YOURMOVE, On the Market and Prime Location. Otherwise expressed as online portals

Along with developing a personal relationship with the estate agents, this is the most successful avenue for sourcing property. Where else can you see the entire market all in one place? You can look at comparables, sold history, the internals of the property and book viewings, all without leaving the comfort of your living room.

A great piece of advice here is that once you've found your investment area (something which I will touch on later in the book) speak with the local estate agents to find out what portals they use for their advertising and be aware that this can, and often does change from town to town.

A prime example here is that in my local town Rightmove is the preferred portal for all the estate agents, but 10 miles down the road they favour On the Market.

I think generally you'll find the less affluent an area is, the more they will use other sites like on-the-market or Zoopla. This is a result of their cheaper monthly tariffs.

Rightmove is the one that I and pretty much every other investor I know predominantly uses, in fact pretty much 90% of my searches are carried out on Rightmove.

The site boasts an abundance of great features to which you can tailor your search quite specifically to meet your individual criteria. You can choose almost any area in the country and set a radius feature to include various surrounding areas by distance.

You're able to specify property type, bedroom quantity, minimum and maximum asking price, view in list or grid form etc. etc.

The more you use the site, the more features you will discover and use.

There are some very useful tools on the site that are particularly beneficial when viewing individual properties.

The map locator can be used to pinpoint the exact location of the property you are considering.

The recent sold history gives all the land registry sold prices for that particular street over the past 20 years or so; this is something that can be used as a comparable tool for assessing an accurate and realistic value of the property you are currently viewing.

It is at this point however, you will need to have a price index chart loaded on your desktop which enables you to see what state the current market was in when the property was sold.

You'll find the index chart for most towns in the UK here at www.home.co.uk

There are many different graphs showing the property price curve within a specific year right back to the mid 90's so it's a great tool to view alongside the 'sold prices' feature on Rightmove as it gives you a firm understanding of the properties current or potential worth.

Another useful online tool that you can use is Googles property tracker for chrome; This is an application that once downloaded is attached to your toolbar on your browser window automatically, this then shows you how long each property has been advertised on Rightmove for. It shows its initial entry and every price or entry change thereafter. It can be used as a great bargaining tool if a property has been advertised for a while. Yes, if you're using an alternative browser like Firefox, then you'll need to switch when viewing Rightmove but you can easily uncheck the default setting when downloading chrome so that it doesn't become your default browser. Firefox used to have their own version in 'property bee .com' until recently, however, this has since been taken down, and as I understand it, there is no plans to reinstate.

Once you're up and running on Rightmove, you can use one of my favourite time-saving features which is their last 24hours, 3, 7 or 14-day search. This feature is so valuable in saving time moving forward since all you need to do after you've spent a good few hours initially trawling through what is available in your chosen area for your chosen budget is to save that as a customised search.

You can replicate this and access that search in 'my Rightmove' but change, within the preferences, to last 24 hours, 3, 7 or 14-days. This way you only need to search every few days to see if there is anything new added to the market that meets your criteria.

Just make sure you keep the original search saved so that you can still keep an eye on the ones that may be struggling to sell. These are the

46

properties that can be picked up below your budget and the current market value, or rather more accurately at the right price.

Rightmove lets you save individual properties into your preference library by simply highlighting the love heart symbol next to the property; this is a great way, along with property tracker of observing the activity of any property.

The greatest time-saving feature, however, has to be the instant notification tool.

If you tick the instant notifications box, you will be sent properties that meet your chosen criteria instantly to your email, thus freeing even more time up to pursue other avenues or other areas of your business.

We get between five and ten emails per day from Rightmove with properties that meet my pre-determined bedroom and price criteria, leaving my staff with the quick and straightforward task of filtering these into the rubbish or potential file using the methods that will be discussed later on in the book.

4) Property auctions

Since the initial airing of TV programs such as 'Homes Under the Hammer' back in 2003, auction houses across the UK have notably increased in numbers, and as a result, more properties are sold at auction, this is a trend that is growing fast, and I don't see any signs of this slowing.

This medium, in my humble opinion, is not particularly good news for professional investors like me.

In my local area, here in the North East of England, it's generally properties that need a good overhaul or entire renovation that are being sold through this medium.

While this can prove to be a good source for finding property especially ones that you can add significant value too It does come with its drawbacks and depending on your strategy, overall aim and budget it can hinder your growth or even leave you with a property that simply isn't right for you as an investor, so be very aware of the implications that are involved.

The big auction house just up the road from me is the Great North Property Auction, and I do from time to time attend their nights, but I have to admit, I have never bought a property at auction nor do I intend to anytime soon.

My investment strategy may differ from others, but I don't like the initial capital outlay, associated fee's and timescales involved.

Like I say though your strategy may be different and as I've just touched on it can be an excellent avenue for securing below market value properties (whatever that is) but as their popularity grows so does their footfall. Herein, for me at least, lies their problem.

The type of investor that now attends these auctions may not necessarily understand the industry as a whole.

Most people attending these auctions are looking for a bargain, or a below market value property commonly referred to as a BMV. The problem here is that the supply and demand balance tips in favour of the vendor which is the wrong direction for us as professional investors.

You may have five inexperienced investors bidding on one BMV property, the result is an overpriced buy for a potential headache of a property and certainly not a BMV.

As I mentioned, there are certain costs involved at auctions, and they do tend to tie more money up in a deal than I would usually like, at least initially.

I will demonstrate a quick example of the costs involved in buying at our local auction house but note: this is not considering the second home stamp duty costs or SDLT as it's known. This was introduced in April 2016 and will be discussed later on. Also, the fees here relate to the Great North Property Auction and may not necessarily be the same in your chosen area

Ok, let's say the hammer falls in our favour and we secure a property for £50,000. Assuming that this is a genuine BMV buy as either the other investors present didn't realise its potential, or they could not attend the auction for reasons we need not go into. It is a safe assumption that this property will be in need of some renovation once contracts are exchanged, and the property is thereafter completed. However, before that time comes and in the here and now the hammer has just fallen, and we are now to pay, immediately a *reservation fee* of £5000 + V.A.T or £6,000.

This fee does not come off the value of the property but instead is added to the value, and I'll note that landlords cannot claim any of the V.A.T back. This is something you need to be very aware of when you are bidding on any property at auction.

Of course, all fees will differ from area to area and between auction houses, so it is imperative that you find this out before you attend as it can alter the purchase price significantly, for example, £6000 on a £50,000 purchase is a 12% increase in purchase price.

So, assuming you've already secured funding of 75% beforehand from your preferred lending method which is the normal procedure, we next have our 25% contribution or deposit to pay.

Based on our example this is £12,500. So, at this point, we have now invested a mere £18,500 on a property that is worth in its present state £50,000, and we now have to renovate. Let's assume that based on an average property of this value and in my experience, the cost of this would be somewhere in the region of £10,000. You have now invested £28,500 in the property, and you have had the hassle of the entire renovation experience. You've had an empty property otherwise expressed as 'lost rent', mortgage payments, council tax bills, energy and water costs and remember this is not taking into account the SDLT on the initial purchase, the solicitor's fees, broker and finance fees and any other associated costs. All of which will be explained in more depth later on in the book.

The fact that I don't think there are many bargains to be had at these auctions anymore due to the high level of interest they incur from part-time investors coupled with the high costs and timescales involved in completion is why I don't like to buy at auction.
I find the cash employed into the deal and the hassle of the renovation all too time consuming and costly.
Something you should note before attending any auction is the terms of the contract which usually state that the deal has to be complete within a specific timeframe, generally within 28-days of the hammer falling.
It goes without saying that generally, this isn't long enough to secure a mortgage on the property, especially if purchasing through the more modern method of limited company acquisitions, therefore it's either pursuing another funding avenue like a bridging loan or a massive cash injection initially ready for refinancing later on.

Your deposit may be lost if the deal is not completed within the given timeframe so be careful and always read the contract or terms of business before you attend an auction.

There is **a counter-argument to the above, however, and it is a good one.**

The property in the example above was bought for £50,000, well, actually let's say £56,000 with the fees attached.

You've then spent £10,000 on renovating and it's now some six months later, you've managed to let the property to a reliable tenant, and the rent is accruing nicely in your account.

This is where it can get interesting.

After owning a property for six months or longer, you are permitted to either mortgage if cash was used initially or re-mortgage if you were able to organise a mortgage in time to initially purchase.

The property will now be revalued for this purpose; there's a good chance you have significantly increased its value due to the renovation and the smart strategy you initially implemented on bidding for the property.

Let's assume that the new valuation is somewhere in the region of £80,000.

You can now release the equity initially employed by mortgaging the property for typically 75% of its total valuation. Therefore, in this instance you release £60,000 in cash, pay back your 75% finance on the £50,000 which was £37,500 which leaves you with the tidy sum of £22,500.

Now, take from this the £6000 auction fee, the £10,000 renovation cost plus your initial £12,500 contribution to the purchase price.

You now have, excluding all solicitors, SDLT and any finance fees etc. for the purpose of the quick example only, a mere £6000 left in the deal and you have a property that is generating somewhere in the region of £6000 a year in gross rent.

This gives you a pretty decent return on investment (R.O.I) or return on cash employed (R.O.C.E). in fact, as a rough guide your ROI would be circa 62%

sounds great huh? Certainly, better than that cash Isa you've got!

There are various ways in which this can work and various methods to purchase the property.

Employing your own savings, joint venturing with a friend or JV partner, using a bridging loan or angel funding and typically a loan leveraged through the more historical avenue of a bank or mortgage company, but I will talk about these in more depth in the strategy chapter of part 1.

Just be very aware of the contingencies as mentioned earlier and go into this with a clear view of what your final goal is. Remain grounded when attending auctions, remember if these deals were truly that good and came along often, there would be an ever-higher footfall at the auction, most likely through professional investors which in turn decreases the chances of securing them further, if this isn't the case, ask yourself why!

For the benefits of the readers, I have demonstrated an overview of the figures in our example, and for the listeners, we will work back over them.

Time to grab a pen and paper, maybe?

Purchase Price	£50,000
Leveraged mortgage contribution at 75%	£37,500
personal contribution at 25%	**£12,500**
Auction fee's	£5000 + V.A.T = **£6000**
Renovation fees	**£10,000**
Total personal capital invested	**£28,500**
Remortgage for £80,000 at 75% LTV	£60,000
Mortgage redemption of £37,500 leaves	£22,500
Minus renovation costs of £10,000	£12,500
Initial mortgage contribution of £12,500	£0
Initial auction fees of £6,000	-£6000
Total invested or locked in the property	**£6000**

A quick disclaimer, although the above demonstration is very likely, the figures used are of a hypothetical nature. They do not represent a previous purchase, they are used for the purpose of that particular demonstration, and they don't include finance arrangement fees, valuation fees, broker fees, loan redemptions or finance charges.The previously mentioned SDLT, council tax, energy and water charges or any prior secured mortgage repayments were all omitted, and of course, they represented a buoyant property market.

5) Professional property sourcing companies

These guys are a relatively new addition to the industry; they scour the property market on a daily basis looking for suitable rentable property or properties that have good scope to increase in value either through capital growth or using renovation as the tool.
They also have many landlords, homeowners and private investors on their books who want quick sales with safe bet investors.
They usually package a deal showing costs involved, comparable properties and general reasoning for their conclusions; they send these deals out through avenues like their website, property forums or group email contacts until someone picks it up and takes a fancy to the deal.

Their fee ranges from town to town and deal to deal, but generally, the fee is a reflection of the deal's potential. For example, a standard single let property that requires a small renovation in order to increase its value making it attractive for refinancing purposes may be packaged at around £2000/£3000, but a large London property that can be changed into an even larger HMO may be packaged anywhere from £30,000 plus.

There are many sites and businesses offering property sourcing across the country so for me to mention them would be a strain on the publisher's ink and also, I don't favour any particular company against another.

As with property auctions I do see their value regarding an introduction to the property industry or if you are a southern based investor perhaps wanting to invest further up north, overall though I am not a big fan of property sourcing for finding deals as I think on the whole their experience and agenda has to be scrutinised.

This view may be slightly contradictory as we do offer this service as a company.

In defence, our market is aimed at our existing clients, mentees or busy working professionals that have come to us through a recommendation, the latter of which are not the kind of people who will be reading this book anytime soon.

If you're investing in an area you don't know, or you have minimal experience in it or in fact in investing on the whole, as in my example above, then my advice is to get reasonably educated before you contemplate implementing any strategy that relies on another source.

Remember that you must always adhere to the five laws of gold, in particular here the 4th Law. As a refresher of that law, it reads.
Gold slippeth away from the man who invests it in businesses or purposes with which he is not familiar, or which are not approved by those who are skilled in its keep.

My main grievance with the sourcing avenue is that is it's another overpopulated area of the property investment industry; it has risen in popularity over the last few years, now it seems every man and his dog has jumped onto the bandwagon. Most of these so-called sources are small-time investors or in fact have no property at all and are using the funds from their deals to purchase their own property investing; this poses a serious ethical issue for me.

How can they advise you on something they either have no or very little experience with? Also, what is their agenda, is it ensuring you get a quality product, one in which can turn your hard-earned cash into sound, predominantly hassle-free investment or is it to get your £3000 to fund their own investing, regardless of the consequence.
Just tread carefully here as most deals are very generic and only really tick the financial box, but as you will see during the course of this book, that simply isn't good enough, there is much more to property investment than purchasing a property below market value, or at a price that ticks a certain yield or ROI, one in which has usually been set by the sources own mandate I might add.

We manage so many properties for smaller investors who have had their entire portfolio sourced for them by an external source, one which they have usually met on a networking evening and in most cases the properties we manage for them; I would not have touched with a barge pole, *a very long one*.

Upon researching this subsection, I came to a forum on the web discussing the topic of property sourcing. The content below is an exact extract taken from the forum that summed up in bullet points, exactly what I thought.

So, here's what was written

- for inexperienced/hands-off / non-full-time investors then it can be very useful - someone else sourcing properties for you could be very beneficial - they will *(most likely)* know more than you and have better contacts, etc
- A property sourcer should be thoroughly researched, however.
- The due diligence that they do for an opportunity is in no way a substitute for your own - always conduct thorough due diligence for yourself.
- If you don't understand the opportunity, don't get involved. No matter what you are told. Be naturally sceptical.
- If the opportunity requires a hard sell, then it's clearly not great - it should be able to sell itself.

- It is almost irrelevant what the sourcing fee is; add the sourcing fee to the purchase price, then run the numbers. If with the sourcing fee, the opportunity is still good and makes sense with your overall strategy then great. So, the actual costs of the property sourcer and the merit of their use is fully down to the actual opportunity itself.
- There is no dark art form of magic to property sourcing - anyone can do it - perhaps not as good as a professional though. Like anything in fact!
- There are lots and lots of great books, magazines, forums, podcasts, etc. that you can educate yourself - so you can make informed decisions based on various sources rather than relying on single sources of info.

I could not have agreed more with the author's points; I think it's summed up perfectly, he was straight to the point and very clearly pointed out the major pros and cons. In essence, I feel there is no replacement for your own research but like he mentioned above and adhering to the 4th law, your own research may entail researching the sourcer and listening to the expert.

This should only be done after you're sure he is going to be as wise with your money as he would be with his own.

This really comes down to your own strategy, whether you plan to invest in your local area or use an expert in your chosen location.

6, 7 and 8) Facebook, friends and family and local landlords' associations

It may please you to find out that I am not so cynical about these avenues, time and time again I have purchased property from the underlining point of this subsection. All the above titles can be summed up collectively and bundled together into one category since they all principally rely on the same underlining point.
Although they can be exclusive in their own right, it really is all about one thing and one thing only, and that is informing people of your intentions and position. Then waiting for the deals to find you.

In the same way as speaking with the estate agents, you're letting people know what you're about and what your intentions are. Contacting the local landlord's associations to introduce yourself and making them aware of your position can be useful since smaller landlords or investors are always looking for quick and easy exit strategies.

Your email or post every few weeks may be placed in a junk folder by many but may just be the very exit strategy that someone is looking for; you'll often find at this stage that older landlords simply want a quick sale for ease of transaction.

Facebook is a great advertising platform and networking tool; you'd be surprised how many people will want to share your intentions if it can help someone they are friends with.

Putting regular posts on Facebook, keeping your work colleagues or clients, friends and family all constantly reminded of your intentions will help your chances of somebody approaching you with a possible sale.

One of the first properties that I purchased many years ago came to me by speaking with my window cleaner one night on his collection.

I had just told him about a property I had just purchased under market value from a client of mine who was retiring and wanting a quick hassle free sale, someone I had been approached by after introducing myself to the local landlord association I might add.

He proceeded to inform me of a parting couple that he happened to clean windows for, he mentioned that she was selling and splitting the money with her fleeting husband and wanted a speedy and therefore cheap sale.

This sale apparently was already secured, but Instead of dreaming, muttering that this would never happen to me, I acted immediately.

Although at this time I only had a few properties, I saw an opportunity and the next day went to the property to post a note to the owner. Upon arriving at the front door, I was greeted by the departing owner, we discussed her situation in some depth, and I left, 25 minutes later with a gentlemen's agreement to buy the property worth £90,000 for a mere £70,000. I was ecstatic at the thought of this, and it just reaffirms my earlier point of action.

It goes without saying that the more you discuss your intentions with as many people as you can, the more chance you have of finding a deal like this, it's simple mathematics, it's the law of probability, the more people you tell, the more chance they will know someone and so on. It helps significantly with your mindset also; you are continually reaffirming your intentions to your subconscious.
Eventually, this will take precedence, and you will become more active on a daily basis as a result.

'A man will become what he perceives himself to be.'
I think this was Mahatma Gandhi but don't quote me on that.

Pun intended!

9) Leaflet Distribution

In my opinion, this medium only has one use, and that is if you intend to purchase the property for under market value and for cash like in the way big firms such as We Buy Any Home do.

Basically, you either mass flyer a chosen area or you approach properties that are already for sale and offer them a chain free solution and a quick no hassle sale.

This method is very time consuming, labour intensive and poor use of your resources. This can work to your advantage once you are an established investor, but for the purpose of a beginner's guide, I do not see it as a credible source.

Enough said!

10) For Sale Boards

It may sound like a ridiculous comment, telling you to search for property using for sale boards, this isn't the 20th century and evidently viewing on Rightmove does that for you right?

Ok, you've definitely got a point. So I am not exactly telling you to leave the comfort of your home, jump into your car and drive around your chosen area all night in the rain looking at for sale boards so that you can jot the address down on a scrappy piece of paper and call the estate agent in the morning. No, but you will find that now your mind is focused on buying property you will see, everywhere you look, for sale boards.

You'll see property in your area from smaller agents who may not be active on the online portal you generally use.

You'll see boards on properties that have just come on to the market that may not be online yet.

You'll see boards on properties that have been there for months on end but you've just haven't noticed them online, or you quickly dismissed it for any number of reasons but in fact you rather like the area or property now that you can see it in all its glory.

There really is no replacement for physical action, going to a property or area to get a good feel for it. In addition to this, it can be an excellent tool for negotiating.

Online sites such as Rightmove may have the following heading '3-bedroom terraced property for sale in Fake Street, Fake Town'.

Now, remember earlier when I told you about the 'recent sold' feature on Rightmove? well, the description above does not say '3-bedroom terraced property for sale **123,** Fake Street, Fake Town'.

You see, you can, once you have the number of the property use this feature to view the initial purchase price and then use this to your advantage.

It gives you some form of leverage when negotiating your price as you can, for the best part and in many cases but obviously not all, assume that they have less than 90% mortgage on this property, and In most cases, depending on the year purchased have much less than this. You can then, once you get an idea of how motivated they are to sell determine what you may be able to achieve as a purchase price.

This is a quick and simple method and can be very useful, but it can't always be relied upon as many variables come into play that determines the vendor's financial position within the property. Variables such as a re-mortgaged or depending on the market they bought in, they could actually be in negative equity with the property. Therefore they have very little motivation to sell below-asking price, but as a general guide, it can prove quite useful. It's defiantly worth having in your arsenal when it comes to negotiating.

In summary to this chapter, it is essential that you form good relationships with the local estate agents as you grow. You should inform every man and his dog of your intentions and position, develop your skills on your chosen online portal and continuously bombard social network sites so that deals come to you rather than having to source them. You need to be very mindful of the risks and costs associated when buying at auction and don't be fooled by the fact that the property needs renovating. You also need to be very aware of what's for sale in, and to rent in your local or chosen location so that you can gauge the suitability of your proposed purchase.

Finally, always question the experience and integrity of anyone trying to sell you the deal of the century.

Part 1 - Getting started
Chapter 2, YOUR chosen strategy.

I intentionally placed this chapter after determining the methods available to source your property for two main reasons. The first is I want you to be aware of realistic property prices within your local or chosen area so that you can then determine your strategy accurately based upon this.

There is little point in coming up with a strategy that allows you to buy ten properties in the first year only to realise that you completely underestimated the value of property in your area and can only buy 3 with your current budget.

Once you have a firm grip on the current market, you can then, using the advice that follows, set out or determine your very own strategy accordingly.

The second reason is that I wanted to ease you in lightly, working out your strategy is crucial to your success and therefore takes great effort and thought, this is not something I would advise a new investor to do alone.

Many years ago, when I got started with property investing there was not a great deal of choice out there, typically you just bought a small fixer-upper and rented it out, job done!

These days the choice is overwhelming with single let properties alone, not to mention houses of multiple occupation (hmo's), serviced accommodation, flats and commercial to residential conversions all thrown in for good measure.

achieving your overall aim or goal buying one single type of property is difficult enough without throwing all these other methods of investment avenues in the mix. Of course, they all have their own individual pulls and drawbacks as well as financial and risk implications to boot.

This chapter is titled '**YOUR** chosen strategy' not 'choosing your strategy 'and certainly not 'how to choose your strategy.'

That might sound like a get out of jail free card, but like I have explained and will continue to explain throughout this book, there are too many variable factors that will determine your own strategy from that of your closest friend, twin brother or like-minded business partner.

I will, however, certainly help guide you through the process, showing you some typical examples of strategies so that you can determine your best course of action effectively.

There are so many variables and determining factors to each, and every one of you that no book or guru can ever tell you, nor should ever tell you what or which strategy to follow, the best any of us can hope to achieve is to demonstrate methods in which you can determine this for yourself.

Galileo once wrote, *"you can't teach a man anything, you can only help him find it within himself."*

To give you a very brief and quick example of some of the differences that will determine or contribute to your strategy I have listed some of the variable factors.

1. **Geographical location** - for example, a strategy in its simplest form in London may be based more around the capital growth of the property while a strategy in the North East of England may focus more on cash flow or ROI as a contrary.
   These are simplified models for demonstrations purposes as both will have, or at least have the potential to have room for either capital growth and or cash flow & ROI, but they will most likely be at opposite ends of the spectrum respectively.

2. **Reason for purchasing** - This is the big one but should be relatively easy to answer, we all want to make money right, but how much, for what purpose and how long are we willing to wait. Is your overall aim to have a single let for retirement purposes, one in which you will save the profit from over the years and use as a lump sum when you retire. Maybe you will use the ongoing rental income to boost your pension after this time or even use the profit initially as a means to

increase your current yearly salary over the next 25 years then use the capital growth of the property to get a lump sum to spend in your retirement. Is it your intention or plan to buy more property on a yearly basis using your savings already accrued as an initial down payment. You then plan to use the rent along with a percentage of your salary until it allows you to buy another property thereafter and so on until the laws of compounding take over and the rate at which you can buy increases exponentially. Do you intend to lifestyle in the industry whereby you buy a below market value property, renovate it yourself at your leisure, sell the property for a small or medium-sized profit or even re-mortgage the property to its new potential giving you the funds to start this whole process again until you have either accrued your desired number of rentals or retirement pot or have enough passive income to replace your current salary. Is your aim to invest money into a business as a special purpose vehicle (SPV) to grow as quick as possible using angel funding finance or joint ventures for your purchases? Do you plan to buy four or five properties from the money a relative has left you in their will, you will buy them all at once and use the rent to either travel around the world carefree or as capital to increase your portfolio on a yearly basis.

I really could go on with fictitious scenarios, but I think you can see many different routes yield many different outcomes which are determined by many different individuals and only you can fully determine your initial strategy as only you know your intentions or desires. I could write hundreds of different scenarios involving a hundred different strategies until I finally hear a voice at the back of the room shout HOUSE, and we are finally on the same page, and yes that pun was intended. Well done if you picked up on both of them. My advice here is to seek the guidance of a professional to help you to determine what is right for you, and I don't mean a generic financial advisor, I mean an expert in property, someone who can really help you through their experience. Financial advisers in my limited experience are generic advisers, but with property, you need a personal tailored strategy.

3. **The amount of capital you have to invest -** This was touched on slightly above, but do you have a large pot of cash to invest in 100% owned properties or in order to use this money as deposits while leveraging the bank's finance to buy an increased volume. Are you currently saving from your annual salary or monthly income until you have enough to buy your first rental? Have you just inherited money or even property from a deceased estate? Do you intend to bridge the loan or go down the joint venture avenue because your finances are the one thing that is preventing you from starting *(I will explain and expand on some of these unfamiliar terms in the 'financing your property' section later on in the book)?* Is your capital tied up in your current property and your partner is a very cautious individual so in order to use this you will need to be sure of some low-risk property

investment rather than the rapid growth high-risk avenue. Do you have surplus funds from your successful business, or do you have a percentage of surplus income that you'd like to work for you since there are only a certain number of all-inclusive holidays you can go on without getting bored of existence!

4. **Do you intend on investing in your local area or are you going further afield -** my next comment could spark a long and arduous discussion by the most successful property investors in the country but would still be full of subjective opinions regardless. However, my opinion is that it is, generally considered to be the safest bet to invest in your local area, and yes this is what I advise you to do initially. I do say initially as this book is intended to give the novice or small-time investor the information required to be able to achieve their own desired result from the industry. I am aware that as you build your portfolio, there may be either the need, desire or you have the financial compatibility to expand your geographical mind. However more than ten years on I still buy within a 20-mile radius from my front door. It is only now that I am starting to contemplate looking further afield. Unless you live in a very expensive part of the country in which case the decision may be taken out of your hands, I would always advise people, especially when starting out to stay local. Starting local can have lots of advantages. You should already have a firm grip on the good or bad streets or roads in your area, the ones you know are desirable locations and the ones you would not drive

down through fear of having your alloy wheels stolen while on the move. You will be aware, to some degree at least of the current trends and price ranges. You can physically drive down through the areas you're potentially interested in to see the competition or the general state of the neighbourhood, and if any significant problems arise from the property, then it's a short journey in a car to help resolve. It may not be feasible for you to invest in your area, however, given the soaring prices in London. One would need a massive amount of capital to buy even one small property, and that may contradict your chosen strategy or long or short-term goals, for example, a cash flow boost. Choosing your location can be one of the most critical factors in determining your success and ensuring that you get this right is paramount. If like a great many landlords across the country you do plan to invest in your local area you must use due diligence and be sure that the maths stacks up and are stress tested against possible outcomes, again I will discuss this later on. If, however, you do decide to invest further afield for a more 'hands-off' investor type of approach, just make sure that the person you trust with this is, in fact, an experienced investor who genuinely has your best intentions at heart. It is even at this point that I would strongly suggest educating yourself on all of the fundamentals of investing so that you can be sure the advice you get from others is true and accurate.

5. **The risk to reward threshold** – Some of you will have sleepless nights over your decision to use standard grade diesel in your brand-new car, and some will have a general que sera sera attitude to life, and your strategies will reflect this and are chanced to be of polar opposites. There are some very safe strategies within property that are low risk, low effort and low investment however it goes without saying that these come with a lower reward also. On the contrary, however, some high-risk strategies also produce high reward. Without wanting to sound like a broken record, only you can determine what your risk to reward threshold is. Generally, this is determined by the type of individual you are but again it is something that can change as investing does get easier and easier the more you do it, and the more you train your mind. If your research is done well, then the risk is always lowered as a byproduct. It's no coincidence that the best investors are also the best researchers and it's not luck that they've done so well either.

   "Luck is what happens when preparation meets opportunity" **Seneca.**

6. **The type of property you're buying -** Are you buying single let townhouses, medium sized new estate type single lets, ex-council estate single lets, four-bed properties to convert into six-bed HMO's or even large commercial properties to convert into residential HMO's. Maybe your buying converted Victorian property style flats,

large block-style flats, fully serviced accommodation, etc.. This list really does goes on and on these days. Each one of these avenues alters your chosen strategy vastly and although there are undoubtedly many transferable factors to each, buying a single let townhouse over a commercial to residential HMO can be very different, especially in financial terms.

7. **Your return** – You may have a pre-determined yield or ROI that you wish to adhere to strictly. You may be flexible with your returns, or they may be paramount to your cash flow. You may be happy to have them slip by the way in exchange for good capital growth. You may not even know what a yield or ROI is yet let alone how to determine them or your cash flow calculation. Well, I can help with that, just keep reading, and all will become clear.

8. **Investor 'v' landlord** – which one is it? I saved this one until last as it's not one that most would differentiate from. Broadly speaking an investor is someone who buys property but does not get involved in the running of the property thereafter, and a landlord is someone who buys a property, organises the tenancy and takes on all of the running of the portfolio. Neither route is right or wrong, and there is some fusion between the routes also. I class myself as an investor but because I run a management company I do cross over into the landlord category slightly. The investor route is far cleaner and is certainly less stressful, but there is perhaps a lower return this way. A

landlord will in most cases yield a better return, but will also become a lot more bogged down with the strains of repairs, chasing tenants etc. It is imperative, right from the start that you understand which route you want to go down as your strategy will have to reflect this from day one otherwise you will ultimately fall into the landlord trap by default.

It may be worth mentioning at this point before we get to the types of strategies available that I am by no means a financial advisor. Before you decide what your best course of action is it may be beneficial to speak with an independent financial advisor for some generic advice. They will help you come up with a plan of attack based on your current financial position and ultimate goal. Just bear In mind that you need to research the type of financial investor you are going to approach. They need to be educated in the field in which you wish to invest, always interview the advisor, make sure they are already on the path you want to follow. I see little point in getting advice from an advisor who is worse off than yourself or rather doesn't invest themselves. it's very easy to preach the ways of the world but to action speaks volume. citing the 5th law of gold from earlier in the book, there are many charlatans out there who will gladly take your money while regurgitating rehearsed information and sound very convincing while doing so. You really want to approach one that is experienced in property investment itself and are themselves financially secure. It is at this point you can get there advice, use it as you see fit & move on up the ladder to a single, specific property type mentor. By doing this, you will be wisely adhering to the 3rd law of gold.

Advice is one thing that is freely given away, but watch that you take only what is worth having. He who takes advice about his savings from one who is inexperienced in such matters shall pay with his savings for proving the falsity of their opinions. Algamish

Determining what strategy is right for you can be the most overwhelming part of property investing, as I have mentioned, there is not already a generic strategy out there that is right for you, every individual will have a different strategy based on their own personal circumstances, aspirations and "definite chief aim" to quote Napoleon Hill. This is something that you simply need to get in order before you start as this will ultimately save time, money and hassle in the long term.

Starting to invest without proper training and mentorship can be costly if your aspirations are long-term security. Every penny spent in the beginning can save pounds in the long run, you're already investing wisely by reading this book and hopefully others to get an overall view of the industry, but I urge you to go as far as your funds can take you with information gathering, after all, knowledge is the key to success. If you would like some sound no-nonsense advice based on years of experience, then please email me at david@wiseowlproperty.co.uk and I can arrange to speak with you over the phone in order to explain the ways in which we can help you come up with a specific strategy that fits your profile, without selling you an irresponsible, generic get rich quick scheme.

Part 1 - Getting started

Chapter 3, Understanding ROI's and Yield's, and their importance

Calculating your ROI or Yield can be very important, and actually, this can be quite fun also, especially when viewing the somewhat desirable outcomes on a carefully designed spreadsheet. I genuinely believe that spreadsheet planning is paramount to property success, it just helps you see all the information, good or bad, in one place. It can be the difference between a good purchase and a poor purchase or a good purchase and an excellent purchase. You have all, well all the financial information at least, there in front of you before you decide to commit. Setting up an interchangeable data input sheet can save time and can help you determine a properties potential in a matter of seconds, this is something I've done right from the very beginning. So, what exactly are Yields and ROI's, I'm sure you'll have heard these terms before, but you may not understand them completely. So, let's explain them in their simplest form then I will get to their importance and, for what it's worth I'll give you my honest opinion on them.

Yield– This term is split or categorised into two different forms. We have 'Gross Yield' and 'Net Yield.' Yields are expressed as a percentage and can be summed up as follows.

Gross yield - this is the simplest form of calculating your yield, it's not as accurate as a net yield calculation can be, but it does give a much quicker calculation which can be used easily in a hurry or on a viewing.

Generally when you hear investors or developers talking about their yields, and they don't specify the expressed yield as a net or gross term, then it is a safe bet to assume that they are talking about gross yield. This is especially true if they sound like they are bragging and even more so if they are trying to sell you something. A gross yield calculation is always expressed as a higher percentage than that of a net yield calculation.

Gross yield is calculated as follows:

First take the amount of rent received in a one-year period, for example, a £650 per month rental has an annual rent twelve times that amount so £650 x 12 months = £7,800 of rent per year. Next divide that figure by the cost of the property, let's say for ease of calculation that we are talking about a £100,000 property.

Therefore, in its simplest term, a £100,000 property at £650 per month or £7800 per year would have an annual gross yield of 7.8%.

That's 7800 divided by 100000 and then multiplying by 100 just to express it as a percentage, and it really is as simple as that, very quick and very easy.

Net yield - this one is a more extensive calculation of the latter. Its main difference is that it takes in to account all the costs associated with running the property, this includes but is not limited to the mortgage, any maintenance, the insurance and/or any agent's fee's that may apply. Therefore the net yield is used more favourably by investors as it's a more accurate way of working out your figures or rather your actual profit from the purchase, although as I'll explain in a short while, I don't really use net yield at all. For the purpose of aiding you, however, and in order for you to make up your own mind, I'll give a clear example based on the above property. That was a £100,000 property at £7,800 rent per year.

The example uses a mortgage payment based on a 75% loan to value mortgage on an interest-only basis at 3.6% which is very easily achievable at the time of writing. A quick check on Google shows we have a mortgage payment of £225 per month, so we have a mortgage cost of £2,700 per year which is to be taken from your £7,800. This leaves you with £5,100, but your agent takes 10% which is another £780 from your £5,100 leaving you with £4,320. Now there are lots of different ways you can continue; some people put in a nominal maintenance fee or a void period percentage but like I mentioned before I tend not to use this. If I did, however, I would just stick to the certainties like mortgage payments and fees, and omit the hypothetical, but possible voids or maintenance figures. So, the example above shows a yield of 4.32% which was worked out from your annual rent minus the mortgage and the agent's fees leaving you with £4,320 to divide by the cost of the purchase, which was £100,000 and finally multiplying that by 100 to express as a percentage as before.

ROI - This stands for return on investment, some people call it **ROCE** or return on cash employed, but in essence, they are one and the same thing. I do tend to use them slightly differently, but that is just my preference. I look at return on investment as the return I get from the money I invested originally, but I look at return on cash employed a little differently. I see this as the return on the cash I have left in the property or deal. So after re-financing or capital growth etc. This does not include the money I have accrued back from rent, however, as that is my cash flow or profit figure. It could be argued that after accruing rent the money you have left in the deal is decreasing so your ROCE is rising at the same rate. But like I mentioned this is just my preference, and it all depends on how strategic you want to be on your spreadsheets and if there are in-fact any benefits to it. Excluding the rent, the return on cash employed gets higher after I remortgage or refinance the property over the years to release equity until I have the option of an infinite return on cash employed.

An example would be if I have bought a genuine BMV, renovated it, remortgaged and then been lucky enough to reap the rewards of a good few years capital growth so that I no longer have any cash left in the deal. My initial ROI may have been 20%, but my ROCE may now be infinite, i.e. I have all my initial money back out of the investment and back in my bank ready to start all over again, yet I still own the cash flowing investment.

ROI is calculated as follows:

Again take the rent accrued over one year, so as per our previous example it was £7,800 per year. Subtract the costs associated with mortgage and management which was £3480 which leaves £4320. Now take the money that you have invested in purchasing and renovating, so this includes but is not limited to, the initial 25% deposit, the valuation and mortgage fees, the SDLT and solicitors fees etc. Let's assume that these all equate to the modest sum of £30,000. The yearly rent is now divided by this investment fee of £30,000 so £4,320 divided by £30,000 and again to express as a percentage, multiply by 100 and our ROI in this demonstration is 14.4%. I know some investors who don't include their mortgage arrangement, broker or even the solicitor's fees in this mathematical equation. It really does not matter what you decide to include or omit, just the same as it doesn't matter when calculating the net yield. All that matters is that you are consistent with your sums every time. There really is no critical percentage for either, just be aware of the actual costs associated with the property. My advice, however, is to include every penny spent on the purchase in order to calculate the correct figure, with the exception of being pedantic by adding fuel, postage and such.

Ok, now you should have a general idea of how to calculate the yields and your ROI. For the benefit of the readers, I will note down the mathematical equations for the demonstrations above. for the listeners, I will read them out clearly. However, it might be beneficial here if you are listening to this on audio to pause in order to grab a pen and paper if all that seemed a little overwhelming.

Gross yield calculation

Annual rent divided by the purchase price

- Annual Rent   £7,800
- Purchase price   £100,000
- Annual rent divide by purchase price   7800 / 100000 = .078
- To express as a percentage   .078 x 100 = **7.8%**

Net yield calculation

Simply explained as the annual profit on the property divided by the purchase price

or

Annual rent, minus the annual mortgage payments, minus the annual management fees then minus any other nominal maintenance or void periods if you chose to do so. Then this sum is all divided by the purchase price

- Annual Rent   £7,800

- Annual Mortgage   £2,700

- Annual Management fees   £780

- Total sum of the fees   £3480

- Annual rent minus fees   7800-3480 = 4320

- Purchase price   £100,000

- Net profit divided by purchase price   4320 / 100000 = .043

- To express as a percentage   .043 x 100 = **4.32%**

ROI calculation

Yearly profit divided by the cost invested in purchasing the property

- Annual Rent   £7,800
- Annual Costs   £3480
- Yearly profit   £4320

Cost to purchase property (broken down)

- 75% deposit   £25000
- SDLT   £3000
- Conveyance   £750
- Brokerage   £250
- Mortgage valuation   £300
    - Mortgage arrangement fee   £700
    - Sum of the purchase   £30,000
    - Profit divide by the costs to acquire   4320/30000 =.144
    - To express as a percentage   .144 x 100 = **14.4%** ROI.

The importance of each calculation and which one to use?

I am aware that some investors use yield as a way of determining their calculations or by means of stacking up the proposed purchase and it is perhaps one of the most commonly misused terms within the property industry. if you watch an episode of Homes Under the Hammer, they can't go 10 minutes without mentioning it, but in all honesty, that's where the buck stops for me.

The reason why these shows use yields is for generic and nonspecific demonstration purposes. You can, without digging too deep into the personal side of someone's investment work out their gross yield in a matter of seconds. Simply take their annual rent and divide it by the purchase price and there you have it, that is why the shows on TV use it. It would be a little intrusive to ask an investor how much of his or her personal cash is tied up in that particular investment and besides it's a much simpler way of demonstration for the masses. Personally, if I hear someone talking about yields, then I either start to slowly shut down, or I assume I am talking with someone who doesn't really understand the property investing game or the laws of money completely.

I view yield as something investors talk about, and I mean stocks and shares, or I've been advised by my broker kind of investors, it's a term used in their world and not the property world or at least the real property world. I never even truly understood or more accurately took the time to work out yields until I was in double figures with my properties, it may not surprise you to hear then, after reading this short paragraph that I quickly dismissed it as a tool for calculating potential investments. When someone talks about net yield, it can have so many variables or costs associated with it.

It may be that your net yield on the same property, with the same mortgage and managed by the same company can still be different from that of your friends or colleagues. Some people get very pedantic and add mileage, wear and tear, bookkeeper fees and any little thing they can so that their calculation is so obsessively accurate that they have truly lost focus of what is really important.

The reason I solely use ROI for assessing a deals suitability is so that I can gauge exactly how well my money is working for me. I can also see how well it's performing in relation to other asset classes, after all, if property investing ever became a poor investment vehicle for me then I would switch to whatever the better option was at the time, for now at least, I'll stick to property.

I can hear a voice in the back of my head saying that they know 6% is a decent yield, they've heard that so many times on TV but never have they heard the term ROI, how on earth am I supposed to know what a good ROI is?

Well again, unfortunately, I can't really tell you that, just like your strategy there are too many variable factors.

This is not me brushing over the subject or sweeping it under the rug. I do intend to help you work this out for yourself, and I will certainly tell you what I class a good ROI as being.

Firstly I don't care how low the ROI is if I have very little cash employed in the deal and the property is in a high capital gain area, for example, London 10 years ago. It bears no consequence since the capital gains would have far surpassed even the greatest ROI's anywhere else in the country. One could argue that as long as the ROI is positive, then it's a good ROI, however, if we are talking a couple of percent, then we would have to hope that there was another influence helping us here, like one of capital growth. If this isn't the case, then 2% can be achieved in the bank, in an ISA or in some low-risk shares etc. so I would tend to look at other avenues.

My dismissive nature to ROI over capital growth comes from hindsight, of course, although you didn't have to be a genius over the last ten years to see that property was booming in London, no one knows what the next ten will hold. In the example above we have the first variable that determines your ROI. Is the chance of capital gains very possible, if so you can, as long as you are breaking even and you don't have all your money tied up, sit back and relax about your pitiful ROI. The counter demonstration is not much capital gain but great cash flow. If this is the case then obviously your ROI needs to be a lot higher to offset the stagnant capital gain. Lastly, we have the happy medium, this is reasonable growth along with reasonable cash flow, this really is the dream but very hard to achieve.

I live in a small town in the North East of England; Capital gains up here is a bit like the government's plan for regeneration over the forthcoming years, non-existent.

I have to rely on a strong ROI, my ROI's are generally somewhere in the region of about 16-26%, but the further down the country you go this should generally reduce in tandem with a rise in capital growth to offset the fall. If I think there is a mixture of capital gain and ROI, then I would reduce this percentage in light of the gains, and this is how you should work out your ROI. I should really keep my mouth closed here since it really is down to the individual to work out their own percentage but again and since I am not a financial advisor nor is this advice in any way meant to be accountable, I would summarise as follows. Up here in the sunny north, I would suggest aiming for as high an ROI as possible, close to 20%. If you are fortunate enough to have a mixture of both gains and good cash flow, then anywhere between 12% and 16% should be a good benchmark and so on as the capital gain likelihood increases. Note if growth slows, not having a contingency can leave you vulnerable.

Part 1 - Getting started

Chapter 4, The three main types of financial strategies

1. Using your own money to fund the entire purchase
2. Using your own money coupled with leveraging
3. Using other people's money or joint venturing

1. Using your own money to fund the entire purchase. This strategy is not for the avid investor but rather the cautious one, the no or little risk, lower reward kind of guy. That does not necessarily mean it's a bad thing, most property investors in the UK have between one and five properties and depending on what your aspirations are in life, your age and your overall goal then this may be the one for you. You're probably don't need to read a 'how to book' to do this, however, because this strategy is generally for the extra cautious you may have purchased this book just to further your education, after all, if I mention one good thing that sticks then I have done my job. Maybe this one small piece of insight was worth the pitiful amount you paid for this book in exchange for the countless hours I laboured writing it. Even though this seems like a straightforward strategy, it can still be further broken down into sub-categories, and this one single area of investment can still have many variables that contribute to different outcomes respectively. This is why I persist with the variable factor mitigation throughout the book.

In our example the investor, Mr Smith has a relatively comfortable lifestyle and has a significant amount of savings to invest in property. The investment is £240,000.

Mr Smith wishes to purchase a single property just around the corner from his own home. Let's assume he lives here in the North East of England. He is probably going to get a five bedroom property with en-suite bathroom, conservatory, large garden, driveway and a detached garage. This property is located in a relatively new and very popular housing estate near to a good school, all in all, it is a very desirable location and will rent no problem.

He will most likely achieve somewhere in the region of £1,000 per calendar month, especially since that nice round figure will aid my mathematical demonstration easier.

The positives here are:

- It's a new style and therefore desirable property.
- It doesn't need any work to get it rented.
- It is providing great cash flow at £900/month which is Mr Smith's profit after his 10% management fees are subtracted; let's remember he has no mortgage to offset on this property.
- The likely hood that the tenants will wreck the property and bolt without paying any rent is significantly reduced due to the level of financial commitment it would take to rent this property initially.

- The property will or should rise steadily in value over the years and the resale of the property, should he require an exit strategy would generally be very quick due to its desirable location.
- It should all in all whilst rented be very low maintenance and hassle-free investment for a while, one in which he can forget about for a good few years.
- He also has the luxury of telling his neighbours he owns a second property most likely very similar to his own just around the corner.

Now the negatives:
- It is a common misconception that the better the property, the better the tenant, ok so I have just commented that there is a reduced chance of wreckage and bolt and I very much stand by that comment, but they are not the only two factors that determine a good tenant. Tenants that pay a higher rent can often be more demanding regarding repairs and expectations. Marks on carpets, creaking doors, painted fences, swelling gates, noisy extractor fans, overgrowing trees, loose patio tiles can all be lived with, repaired by the tenant or complained about. Generally, in the higher price rental market, the consensus can be " I'm paying all this money every month, I want a five-star service, and I want it now".
- Remember the description, remember the large garden, drive, detached garage, conservatory, they all sounded ideal. Well these are all hindrances in void periods or as the property increases in

age, conservatory windows mist, moss grows on drives, garage doors seise, the grass needs mowing during void periods or the tenants let it overgrow constantly and therefore aiding weed growth.

- It goes without saying that the more expensive the property, the more expensive it is to maintain, principally a large five-bed detached property will cost more than twice the amount to re-paint and re-carpet but will wear at the same rate as a three-bedroom terraced property.
- Lastly, and only in my experience through the lettings business these properties are on a shorter term let since they are either relocating professionals, couples wanting to rent until they find their own property or in some cases, they have overestimated the costs and efforts of running a larger property.

All said and done buying a £240,000 property is a great achievement and should not be underestimated. The many variables above can go either way, and they are only there to show you some quick examples. You may find that all positives prevail and the tenants stay for ten years, they improve the property and never call to report any problems.

In our second example, Mrs Jones also has £240,000 to invest. She buys three properties all valued at £80,000. Again here in the North East, she would get three bedrooms, mid terraced properties achieving about £550 rent per calendar month each. This equates to £1,485 in total for all three after her 10% management fees are subtracted. Remember she bought these properties for cash, so again there is no mortgage to offset here.

The positives:
- She gets a higher cash flow totalling an extra £585/month which equates to £7,020/year or £70,200 over a ten-year period. Obviously, these examples are idealistic scenarios; it would take us into the depths of the abyss to start to cover likely void periods or repair costs etc.
- the properties are smaller and don't have large gardens, conservatories, garages etc., so they are a little easier to manage in terms of unnecessary or unwanted maintenance
- The tenancies tend to last longer, and rent can be increased at the same rate but spread over three properties, so the return gets higher on each incremental increase.
- She owns three properties so selling one to free money up for something else does not leave her without a cash flowing investment.

95

- Again, she has the luxury of telling her neighbours that she has multiple properties as investment vehicles.

The negatives:
- It goes without saying that by owning three rental properties it is going to be harder to achieve a 100% occupancy rate than owning just one.
- There is a higher risk of non-payment of rent and wreckage or damage to the property since the level of tenant they will attract generally tends to be of higher risk. Although I do intend on demonstrating later on in the book how to reduce this risk dramatically.
- Owning three properties means you're about three times more likely to have a boiler breakdown, higher risk of leaks or electrical failures or any other repairs for that matter.

Generally, though over the course of a ten-year period, as you can see above, you will be better off financially. The example shows there is a higher risk in tenants and repairs, but then like I explained risk generally goes hand in hand with reward and my expert advice later on in the book will alleviate a lot of the 'risk' associated with housing so-called 'bad tenants'

Investing your own money outright on a purchase is a very safe option but depending on your overall goal, hassle factor tolerance, return on investment expectation and overall approach there are still many ways you can attack this. I'm sure whichever way you choose to proceed you'll be left happy with approximately between £108,000 - £178,200 in potential gross rent over a ten-year period plus some capital growth that's undoubtedly more appealing than having the money sat devaluing in the bank. These figures are based on the example above.

2. Using your own money as well as leveraging a loan. This is perhaps the most common type of investment strategy; it's certainly the one that's used predominantly in my strategy.

Typically, it's using your own money coupled with a loan or mortgage from someone like the bank or a specialist mortgage lender.

In most cases, it's 25% from your savings pot and 75% from the bank or mortgage company. The term we all use here is leveraging whereby you leverage someone else's capital to get your desired outcome, I.e. you leverage the funder's capital to buy a £100,000 property when you only have a £25,000 deposit.

Obviously, this means you can buy more properties or higher value properties than you could without adopting this leverage.

This is the most common type of strategy used by smaller investors as in most cases it's the only method that they are aware of.

Again though, this single strategy can be widespread and varies from investor to investor.

This variation relates to more than general terms like the value of the property or leveraged loan. It can be the mortgage type or term, the amount of valve you can add to the property after purchase for re-mortgage purposes, the intention in using your current funds then ceasing to invest or to refinance to leave less of your 'cash in the deal' to help you buy more properties over and over and eventually compounding as you grow.

It's not my job here to give you a demonstration of each strategies variable factor, since there are so many, but rather give you an overview of how the 'leveraging' strategy works.
With that in mind, I will demonstrate for those who aren't already three steps ahead here, a quick example.

The example will be based on the investment amount in point 2 from this chapter as well as the property value from the same example.
I am sure you understand by now how to work the figures out for yourself based on different value properties, the formula is the same it's just the inputs that are different.

So, we have £240,000 to invest, and we are buying properties around the £80,000 mark.
Again, for the ease of calculation, we are not considering legal fees, SDLT etc.
I will go into some depth with this later on in the 'purchasing' chapter of the book.

Ok, so we need to put down £20,000 per property for our 25% contribution, that enables us to buy 12 properties all renting at £550/month or £495/month after subtracting the agent's fees. Although I'm quite confident that if you were to hand 12 properties over to an agent for management, they would offer a decent reduction in their overall percentage and if they don't, and unless you think their value is worth their charge, look elsewhere.

If they don't want your business then maybe that tells you how hard they will work for you if they get it.

It is at this point I will take another very small but relevant detour. 10% of your rental income may not sound like a large amount but over the course of a mortgage term and multiplied by 12 properties it soon ads up.

12 x £55 is £660/month which is £7,920 per year or £198,000 over the term of the mortgage, not taking into account rent inflation and other costs.

This £198,000 may be better wrote as another nine properties with change. this, in turn, adds more rent to the pot compounding as it goes, and this compounding does grow exponentially so, in reality, the properties you could add to your portfolio would be more than nine even when taking into account your mortgage payments.

Now it may be worth considering your options here in terms of self-managing. I've always self-managed, and through that, I gained the experience and knowledge I needed to open my own lettings business. This now means my properties are effectively managed for free and at the same time adding another revenue stream to my portfolio.

Now, with the training courses we offer and my newly acquired hobby of writing, I have multiple streams of revenue, and all within the same industry, meaning my focus is not diluted but instead magnified.

So, back to my example.

We have 12 properties bringing an assumed £495 each in rent per month; this is based on an interest-only mortgage of 3.5% which is more than achievable in the current climate.

Now, your repayments would be circa £175/month for each property leaving you with a rental cash flow of £320 on each one.

So, Your monthly cash flow is £320. When you times that by 12 months it equals £3,840 each or £46,080 every year combined 'or' expressed as £1.152 million pounds over the 25-year mortgage.

Again this is excluding all associated maintenance and void costs which will be discussed later in the book.

Excited? you should be AND, it gets better, a whole lot better.

Remember the wonderful law of compounding that I've mentioned a few times, the one that Albert Einstein himself called the 8th wonder of the world, well this is the exciting part.

So this one is quite difficult to explain without a pen and paper, and we do go over this in some depth on one of our training course but, in essence, if you re-invest the capital from the first year, you're then in a position to acquire (using leverage), another two properties.

This elevates your rental income from £46,080 to £53,760 in the next rental year or better exemplified as £1,290,240 over the remaining 24 year period. Now if you carried on re-investing that income periodically, you can sit back and watch the funds compound on this ever-increasing exponential scale to a point where you probably won't be able to keep up with it.

It is at this point you see the figures just become silly, very silly.

But before you keel over, wet yourself with excitement and quit your job we must remember that not everyone has £240,000 to invest initially.

It would be a fair bet that the majority of people reading this book will have very little to invest, and those of you that do will most likely have nowhere near that figure so discussing using other people's money as a vessel to invest will certainly be of interest to you.

4. Using other people's money.

Really? Using other people's money, is this real, what's the catch and is this something anyone can do?

Well yes, it is very real, there is a small catch, and yes you better believe that almost anyone can do this.

There are different ways to use someone else's money to buy property, and not in the way we leverage the bank's money to buy a large asset with a smaller portion of our own money, although we can also do this through this vessel.

This can be a JV or joint venture partner or through the use of a bridging loan, angel finance or any of the other imaginative wording used to describe borrowing money in the short term.

This method is becoming increasingly popular these days for many investors, both new to the market investors with no initial capital or with established smaller investors who have proven track records but have run out of personal funds to leverage.

There are many courses run throughout the country that teach this whole process, but I will briefly explain a few different ways so that you can understand more clearly enabling you to decide if this approach is something you would like to pursue further.

Joint venturing or a JV partner, this can run a number of different ways and often depends on the JV partner themselves as to how it's set up and subsequently ran, after all, they are often the ones in the driving seat as they have the available funds. You can JV with a friend or family member or with a JV partner you've met through a networking event, or training course and all will be run or set up, usually as a reflection of your relationship.

Joint venturing with a friend. Let's say that you can both, with some effort get hold of £10,000 each but it is about the full exertion of your funds meaning you really couldn't buy a reasonable property individually.
However, by coupling your savings together, you are able to raise the 25% deposit needed to obtain a decent, cash flowing rental. You can then use the income plus the income you can both add from your employment or other avenues to save another £10,000 each and start the process again.
This way you are leveraging each other and the bank at the same time to get what you desire. The whole process of raising the £10,000 becomes a little faster this time around since you have the rental income from your first property.
Now the cash flow injected into the pot comes faster once again as you have income from property no.1 and no.2.
This then increases once more and so on until before you know it raising £10,000 each is a simple process of time rather than saving.

This example can be a slow way to build a portfolio initially, but it is an effective way to get onto the property ladder quicker rather than trying to save the entire deposit yourself.

This is a beneficial approach since it has the ability to take earlier advantage of any capital growth and starts the whole process of cash flow faster.

After all, as I have explained waiting for the time is right, or until you have the funds may never come at all. We all know how life can get in the way of even the best thought out plans, as advised earlier in the book, start now, and if this is the only route then great, what's stopping you, it's a very safe low-risk option.

The second option would be to Joint venture with a business partner. Generally, someone, you have either sourced or been put in touch with through a networking event or JV site or course. This route, in some cases, can enable you to leverage the JV partner's money 100% so, in essence, it is the purest form of 'no money down'.

With bank interest rates currently as low as they are and have been for some time now, having money sitting in bank accounts, even premium accounts makes no sense for wealthy businessmen.

They are always looking for ways in which to get a better return on their capital, and you can be their knight in shining armour.

In essence, you do all the leg work in sourcing, viewing, calculating, compiling and then presenting the deal. Once this is accepted, and the finer points of the share deal are ironed out you deal with the agents, solicitors, renovation if necessary, the utilities, advertising, finding the tenant and managing thereafter.

Note that the last couple of points can be leveraged further with the JV partners consent by employing a suitable management agency.
The role of the JV partner here is simply to stump up the full amount required for the purchase, you then profit share either 50/50 or whatever the terms of the contract states thereafter.
He gets a hassle-free semi guaranteed ROI, and you get a property without expenditure.
It is worth mentioning that there are many different ways this can work in terms of ownership, profit share etc., the main drawback to this is that the JV partner is generally in the driving seat when it comes to the negotiations so don't expect an easy ride.

Bridging loans, angel funding or other such ways of borrowing money in the short-term.
Like I've just explained this is a short-term loan usually about 8-12 months since the money laundering laws prohibit anyone from mortgaging or re-mortgaging a property within six months of the initial purchase. By the time the T's are crossed and the I's are dotted on the re-mortgage it generally has taken between 8 and 12 months after the initial purchase. This is a great way to get onto the property ladder if funds are scarce or even pretty much non-existent.

I would say that these last two methods of investing are the best-kept secrets within the property industry, I have not met many people over the years who are not already property investors that are aware you can purchase property without having capital.

This method does come with its drawback or catch, however.

It is a costly way to borrow money; most lenders will charge either a fixed fee for a period or high monthly interest payments.

You will be responsible for all the costs involved in setting up the contracts and the loan, and some funders will even charge their own administration charge when the loan is repaid.

That all said, this is becoming a more popular method for investors, so the terms of these loans are becoming a little more competitive now.

My advice here is to speak to more than one lender, in essence, you may need to change your approach or mindset when pursuing this avenue.

Yes these guys are lending you a vast sum of money, and you need to present yourself as a suitable candidate, one that is risk-free, experienced and confident in approach but you also need to remember that you are making them money, they want your business just as much as you want their money.

Without this parallel, these guys would not have the revenue stream so, in essence, you are interviewing each other. Always remember that this is a mutual arrangement, although they are lending you a vast sum of money they are certainly not doing you any favours by making so much money from you at the same time.

So how does it all work? I hear you say, well I am glad you asked! Ok so straight to the point, and by means of a quick overview as this avenue really does need further research by the individual.

You will find a property that you're interested in, one that you know you can add value to by renovating or extending its scope, you then present the figures of your finding to the lender, they agree, and you both iron out the contractual agreement until he releases the capital. This capital is either an outright purchase or the funds for a mortgage; you purchase the property, renovate it in order to increase its value, rent it and six months later mortgage the property at the higher value. The money comes through from the new lender, and your bridging loan is settled. Any capital left over after completion is yours.

A quick note to say that the lender will in most cases put what is called a first charge on the property. This is something mortgage companies also do; it means that until the charge is lifted the funds from any sale go directly to paying back his loan first before you see a penny, it is by means of security that they do this.

This method can work very well for you if you can find a property that is below the current market value, one in which you can add significant value to by means of renovation. A quick example of how this works in monetary terms is as follows:

You source and buy a property for £50,000; it has the potential to achieve £80,000 - £90,000 once extended or renovated fully.
You spend £10,000 on the renovation process, so you have borrowed £50,000 and spent £10,000.
The property sells or is mortgaged at £85,000 thereafter
You mortgage the property at a 75% loan to value or LTV meaning you acquire £63,750.

The bridging loan plus fees are paid back, and the result is you walk away from the deal with none of your money left in the property or owing to the lender, therefore, owning a property for free and with a return on cash employed expressed as an infinite number.
Pretty good huh?

Now obviously with the rise of education finding these properties is becoming harder, but there is no need to find one with such high gains, it just means that you are left with some of your own money left in the property.

Still, if you walk away with £7-8k tied up in the property, it's certainly a great option and a fantastic ROI or ROCE.

This is a very popular approach for those wanting to build a portfolio of their own rather than joint venturing, remember this was you can own the property 100% rather than 50%. Conversely, you can adopt this approach with a JV partner. In a case where you both want to invest but don't have the capital even after coupling your savings this is a viable option to pursue.

Part 1 – Getting started

Chapter 5, Interest only V's repayment mortgages

As we have previously discussed the most typical mortgage available for a buy to let purchase is a 75% loan to value. This means that the lender, being a bank or mortgage company will loan you up to 75% of the total value of the property or 75% of the figure that their own sourced valuer indicates the property is worth.

In real terms, this isn't always the purchase price, although in my experience on lower value properties, say under £100,000 there aren't usually many discrepancies, none of any significant value anyway.

If the lenders over cautious valuer and trust me when I say they are under increased pressure from the lenders to be so values the property under the purchase price you have a few options.

The first option you have is to bite the bullet, take the small financial hit (usually a few hundred pounds for a valuation fee) and switch mortgage companies in the hope that you'll get a value that is more realistic or on par with the purchase price or agents' valuation the next time around.

It is worth mentioning that any good broker will be able to tell you which lenders are stringent, and which are usually on par when it comes to their valuations.

The Second option is to put in the extra funds yourself;
The lender will still offer you 75% of their scrupulous valuation. So if you've agreed on a purchase price of say £100,000, but the lender's valuer values the property at £90,000, then you would have to make the difference up yourself.

Your deposit on £100,000 would have been £25,000 as the valuer would have lent you 75% therefore £75,000 but their over cautious and scrupulous valuation means they will lend you 75% of £90,000 which is £67,500 so now your deposit or contribution would be £32,500 in order to make up the purchase price, this is an increased deposit of £7,500.

Word of caution, however, if the valuation on the property does come in lower than the purchase price, especially by the amount in the example above then it may be wise and an appropriate response to do some further research just to ensure that you feel confident that the property is actually worth the agreed purchase price.
Although I don't condone pulling out of deals, I also appreciate that other peoples' financial circumstances may differ from mine and, although the due diligence should have been done initially, it now may be the best course of action.

Alternatively, or the third option here is to approach the vendor and negotiate a discount based on the valuation and their findings, this is obviously the desired outcome. I have recently done this myself, the value of the property came back £3000 lower than my agreed purchase price which I knew was a good buy anyway. The valuer, who lives out of the area indicated a lower figure than the agreed purchase price so I returned to the agent and informed them that we could only proceed at the newly valued price. Result, this is perhaps the only time I will ever thank the bank's valuer, as this time it worked well in my favour.

I will explain the whole negotiation process in a little more depth later in the book. For now, we will get back to the point of this chapter, Interest only 'V's' repayment mortgages.

So, for the complete novice, in layman terms and by no means wishing to patronise or teach anyone how to suck the proverbial egg.
A repayment mortgage pays the complete value of the loan down over the term of the mortgage including the agreed interest on the loan. This is typically a 20-25-year period depending on your age and circumstances, shorter or even longer terms are available and are sometimes the only option, but this is generally circumstantial.
On the last day of the mortgage, in 20-25 years' time, depending on what term you went for initially you will make your last payment and have no subsequent money owing on the property. The lender will release the first charge held on the property, and you are now free to do as you wish. Reap a greater monthly income, sell the property or in some cases remortgage once again.

With an interest-only mortgage, you pay the agreed 'interest' on the mortgage on a monthly basis, and that is it. When the term of the mortgage is up after 20-25 years, you still owe the lender the full amount that was initially borrowed, i.e. 75% of the purchase price.

It goes without saying that they both come with some attractions and some drawbacks. Now depending on your individual strategy, you may decide to go one way or the other or even a mixture of both throughout your portfolio, but before you decide, let me shed some light and give you my opinion.

The repayment type mortgage is usually the choice of the more cautious investor.

Generally speaking, investors that are buying property as a retirement pot or little boost of income in line with their primary job go down this route.

It is, unless funds are limitless a far slower way to build a sizeable portfolio, but if building a portfolio slow and steady for longer-term gains on a more solid foundation is your aim then this is an excellent choice.

Just because it is deemed a more cautious approach does not mean that you can't make a great deal of money this way.

I started my portfolio in precisely this way and still to this day hold some properties on a repayment basis, albeit only a few circumstantial ones.

It is also a great way to lower your LTV percentage across your portfolio.

The concern for the more modern investor is that the mortgage fees are much higher on a monthly basis due to the repayment element. This means your cash flow each month is lower, this in-turn takes longer to accrue the funds to start the whole process again. Albeit the strong counter-argument to this is that someone else is paying the mortgage down for you over the term. If you have void periods however then this can have a bigger impact of capital until the property is re-let meaning that you may be under increased pressure throughout the term to meet payment demands from the lender or your profit can be squandered faster during these void periods.

The interest only method is a much faster, more aggressive and slightly higher risk strategy which like I've just mentioned leaves you with a lump sum to pay at the end of the fixed mortgage term. However, it does have some significant benefits to boot.

Firstly and as I have just touched on the monthly payments are far lower since you are only paying down the interest on the loan each month or year. This now means that you accrue a more considerable sum of surplus cash on a faster basis, in-turn the balance in your account builds quicker as a result. This again compounds the more property you own, and the more funds you accrue. The faster you can buy another property the better regarding cash flow and repetition.

This is exciting for investor's especially professional investors who aim to run this like a business or wish for the property industry to give them the flexibility and freedom no job can offer.

Buying property this way enables you to build your portfolio at a faster rate or have a better short-term lifestyle since the returns are far more attractive.

I will use this opportunity to demonstrate a quick example of an interest-only loan over a repayment type.

Let us say that the purchase price is £100,000 at a 75% loan to value. I use £100,000 since the figures are always easier to demonstrate for ease of explanation.

I will again omit all the associated costs and fees attached to the mortgage, as promised I will explain these in depth later on in the 'buying' section of this book.

Both interest only and repayment mortgages require you to use £25,000 from your own funds. Therefore, the leveraged loan amount here is £75,000.

Although there are better rates available and a good broker will help you achieve these I've based this demonstration on approximate current mortgage interest rate of 3.75%.

This rate has been obtained through a quick search I've just run on Google, *other search engines are available but let's face it, they are inferior.*

The monthly payment on a repayment type mortgage would be £386 per month but based on an interest only mortgage the repayments significantly reduce to £235 per month. This is of course for the fixed term specified within the mortgage offer, this is usually 2-5 years fixed but you can always negotiate a new deal towards the end of this fixed period, and sometimes there are no costs involved either especially if you are staying with the existing lender.

Remember that if you don't negotiate a new deal, then it is at this point that your mortgage will change to the lender's current rate but bear in mind for my demonstration that the relative difference between the two payments will still be somewhat the same.

You can see from the example above that the difference in payments between the two mortgages types is £151 per month which, all being well, equates to £1,812 per year, remember this is the extra amount you'll receive between the two payment methods, not the amount you make. Now, this figure is a noticeable difference in profit that reflects well in your account when you own a single property, but when you own multiple properties, this figure becomes more significant.

Let's imagine you have the £100,000 property on an interest only mortgage over a 25-year term and the rent is £600 per calendar month.

Based on an idyllic scenario of full occupancy and no major repairs beyond your remit, you can hope to achieve £4380 in pre-tax profits each year on this property.

Now couple that figure with the second or subsequent property of equivalent standing and you can see that it won't take long to accrue the kinds of funds needed to either buy another rental, have a greater lifestyle or even replace your current employed income.
Obviously, the main drawback to the interest-only route is the lump repayment sum in 20-25 years' time.

This can be damming if your repayment in 20-25 years comes at a time when the property market is at an all-time low or has, in fact, crashed beyond expectation.
This is something you need to be very aware of but then, dare I say it not really, once in fact, you are aware!

Ok, so I'll explain that last mitigation. There is a twist to the decision, and it is a big and exciting twist one which, in my mind sways the pendulum well in favour of the interest only route.

When I first started investing years ago, being from a typical working-class northeastern family, it had been ingrained in me throughout my youth to work hard, save for the future, don't buy or spend unless you can afford or really need to, and definitely, under no circumstances do you get into debt.

It might not surprise you to hear that my first few mortgages were on a repayment term. I even overpaid on the repayments at the maximum permissible rate without any redemption charges being applied to my account. I did all the repairs, renovations and improvements myself on an evening or weekend after work and I only bought more property when my deposit was saved up, slowly and even then only when I had a big enough contingency set aside thereafter.

I was overly obsessive with getting the elusive "undervalued" properties and as you may recall in the first chapter that years later these properties were not so undervalued anymore. The whole BMV or below market value saga requires comprehensive debate.

It goes without saying that this was a long and slow process for someone who at that time had a decent income. I don't look back and regret the way I did things after all my upbringing governed the way I invested, I nearly didn't invest at all through caution, and again I don't begrudge my upbringing, both factors contributed in their own way to the modern day me.

My upbringing gave me great financial sense and respect for the value of money and my initial approach to buying property gave me a solid foundation for future growth; I could even argue that it gave me a better foundation for rapid growth.

That aside if I knew what I know now about the industry I would have been a lot further on than I am, even now. But then wouldn't we all with the added benefit of hindsight and gained knowledge.

A couple of years into my slow and part-time, makeshift property buying adventure I bought two properties simultaneously off an existing and retiring client of mine. I was able to do this since I purchased them with a good friend at the time and now a very successful business partner.

We now own together, an investment company investing predominantly in HMO and commercial properties but back then these were my 3rd and 4th properties respectively.

Steven was at the time and still is all about cash flow, build the pot quickly and aggressively and worry about the future later, take the rewards while they are on the table and cross the proverbial bridge when or even if you ever come to it.

Now, this mindset back in the day worried me greatly as I'm sure it will a great deal of you too, but Steven had convinced me to put these properties on an interest-only mortgage. If I didn't need his half of the capital at the time to buy the properties, as there was no way of splitting the sale, I am pretty sure I would have walked from the deal.

At the time it was an excellent opportunity to purchase two well-undervalued properties, a small chuckle to 'undervalued' here, so I went for it. I then went back to my old way of investing in repayment type mortgages and making overpayments when I could.

I now felt like I had a balance within my expanding portfolio, a couple of cash generating properties and all the others on a repayment basis, a low LTV and some cash flowing in. Now, this was and still is today a great lower risk strategy that I am sure some of you will adopt and will do very well in doing so.

For me, some years later after reaping the cash from these two interest-only properties the penny finally dropped.

I was talking with a colleague at one of the few networking events I attended in early 2009. I had just bought a repossession for the modest sum of £35,000 and had to pay cash to get this deal through as no mortgages on property of this value were available. I remember his exact words were "wow I remember how much money £35,000 was when I was 30 years old, it doesn't seem that much these days huh?"

It took me a minute of silence and careful pondering, but I asked him his age. He told me he was 49 years old. This comment got me thinking about money and the differences in amounts from one generation to the next due to increases in inflation.

Later when I returned home, I did some research to gauge property prices 20-25 years ago, and how much I would have to pay back in say 25 years. Yes, you guessed it, the term of a mortgage.

Yes, I had to buy this property for cash because my broker, at the time could not source a buy to let mortgage at this value, but you better believe me when I tell you that seven and a half months later when I mortgaged this property, it went on an interest-only mortgage.

You see what I had realised, finally and most likely well after everyone else is that inflation pays down the cost of the loan amount for you. or rather it erodes the value of the debt.

This is the exciting part for investors. When this mortgage is due in 25 years' time, the amount of money leveraged which was £48,750 won't reflect anywhere near today's value of £48,750 but rather and presumably an insignificant sum in comparison.

A prime example of this using history as a tool would be:
let's say we purchased a property in 1975 for the UK average of approximately £9,000 and placed this on a 25-year interest-only mortgage so it would be due its completion right on the turn of the millennium.

Let's assume that we, as we do today leveraged 25% of the bank's money to purchase this property. It is at this point that the owner of the said property will have to find £6,750 to settle the loan. Now in 1975, a £9,000 property would be the approximate equivalent of an £80,000 property in today's market.

Finding £6750 in the year 2000 and according to the office for national statistics would have been approximately equivalent to one-third of the average annual wage in the UK.

Its safe to say that the majority of investors will have a higher income than that of the national average.

I personally in the year 2000 aged only 20 years old was earning somewhere in the region of £24,000, so the redemption of the mortgage in our example would have been equivalent to a little over three months' pay.

If this trend continues as it repeatedly has time and time again through history then finding the money to pay back 75% of the £80,000 interest-only mortgage without selling the property shouldn't pose too much of a problem in 25 years time.

I don't think I need say much more about the powers of inflation with respect to eroding the value of your mortgage.

I often think that given my time again with a more privileged start to investing whereby I had more capital to invest immediately in property without having to accrue further funds I would still like to remain a little cautious and spread the eggs by having a percentage split between interest only and repayment. However, my investing cap gets thrown back on, and it brings me back down to reality and the point of being a professional investor which is to buy property as fast as is reasonably participle, without being foolish and adopting a sound well thought out strategy of course.

The reality is, given my time again with the knowledge I have gained to date I would always opt for an interest only product.

Obviously, everyone is different, and it takes a particular person to reach certain heights, and if you know in your heart of hearts that this is not you then I would urge a more cautious approach initially, you can always adapt at a later point.

The reasons I do what I do and choose how I choose are far different from your reasons.

I hope this chapter has given you some insight to help you understand the differences in the potentials and pitfalls of the two main mortgage types available to us all.

It would be wise at this stage to work out your overall goals, objectives, aims, and risk to reward feelings.

You must bear in mind your current financial position and talk to as many professional investors as possible, not your parents, cautious friends or dog, unless of course, with the exception of the dog they are professional investors. Always seek advice from the people you are trying to emulate or that have qualities you don't but do desire.

If your dog is a professional investor, please do get in touch as I feel we could help each other increase our wealth significantly!!

Part 1 Getting started

Chapter 6, Refurb or not to refurb that is the question

Before we move on to part two of this book I want to talk about refurbishing or renovating property briefly; I want to help you further understand the implications and hopefully put your mind at ease with the daunting task of property development.

I have talked with many people over the years and the one thing that keeps cropping up, more often as an excuse is that they are no good with their hands or that, in the early days for me "it's ok for you, you can do all the work yourself". This comment really annoys me; I started out in this industry with little knowledge, I made many mistakes, and it took me a long time to figure things out and develop the understanding or strategy I employ today.

Although the internet was full steam ahead when I started investing, the information wasn't as abundant, widespread, credible or as easily accessible as it is now, and I certainly did not use it to anywhere near its full potential so I should maybe have a little patience with this next comment, **but, it is just an excuse**.

That's the main bug bearer for me, it wasn't all right for me because I could do the work myself, I haven't done that for many years now, and I still survive.

I suppose what they really mean is that:

"it all sounds ideal, and if someone put it on a silver platter for me so that I don't have to get off my arse and educate myself on the intricacies of property investing, I might then consider it. Even then it is outside of my comfort zone so I would probably be too reserved to take the step anyway, but at least in 10 years' time I can tell people down the local pub about the one that got away or when I nearly bought a property to rent out".

To be honest, if someone actually made the above comment, they would immediately gain my respect rather than using the prefix of an excuse that its ok for me which comes from their belief that they feel they should try to reach common ground by patronising, insulting and discrediting my hard-fought achievements.

Wow, harsh! Yes, I know, but you meet very few people in this life who really speak their mind, their true mind I mean, who really think about what they have to say and only say what they feel is right.

Not investing in property because you're not DIY minded a ridiculous notion, there are better investors out there than me, and I would guess that the majority of them are far worse at DIY.

I am not the greatest accountant in the world, that's why I employ an accountant for my business.

I cant source mortgage products, that's why I employ a broker, I'm at a complete loss when it comes to conveyance, that's why I employ a solicitor, and I cant build websites, so I employ a graphic designer.

The point is if you can't manage tenants or the DIY just add it to the business plan as a business cost. The figures will still stack up, albeit a little smaller, but don't use the ridicules notion that if you were better with your hands, then you would invest because you wouldn't. Instead, you'd find another excuse!! Property investment is not about fixing problems in houses.

Ok, tangent rant over and back to the point of this chapter, refurb or not to refurb.

This book is designed as a guide to help you figure out your own specific strategy, and it's not a step by step guide on the development of my own sporadic whirlwind of a strategy, if it was you'd have put it down a long time ago amongst a mass of confusion, contradiction and incoherence.

I will of course, as in previous chapters tell you what I do, did or how I invest now, on the whole.

It is not for the purpose of replication however, but instead meant as a way of not shirking my obligation as an author of a book on property investing.

So many times, have I read books that fail to deliver on so many fronts due to the author's reluctance to share his true thoughts.

I sometimes renovate fully, I sometimes refurbish, and I sometimes buy and rent straight back out since the property is in a very rentable state already.

I've bought recently renovated properties before. Ones in which another investor had made his money by buying low, renovating fully and selling to either get his money back out to start again, buy other rentals himself, take his wife to the Bahamas or because he didn't realise how desirable the location was, either way, we both won.

The point is it doesn't matter if the property needs a full renovation of £20,000 a smaller refurbishment of £5000 or is in an immaculate condition. What really matters is that the maths makes sense fundamentally. You can then apply the other factors secondary to establish the properties suitability.

Unless your strategy deems that you must add value to the property or you need to purchase the property for as cheap as possible in order to complete due to lack of readily available funds and the other discussed options are not viable then it bears no difference. Your strategy, as I have mentioned should adapt and develop over time just like mine has.

I mentioned earlier in the book that my strategy these days is all about simple mathematics and not so much about the individual circumstances. I'm not sure if this is because I am at a stage now where the smaller details do not matter so much as there are far less financial implications or overall consequences or because I am that good at sourcing property that it is just second nature to find the right deal.

Whatever the reason is I do base my searches for my own property more around the mathematics, despite my grievance with sourcing companies doing this. I would note for the record that I would never outsource a property in this way, I always look at the entire picture in this instance, possibly I do anyway subconsciously anyway as I tend to invest in areas I am very familiar with.

Let us assume that you see a property in your local area, again I will use my local investment area as the example.
The property is for sale for £65,000, but it needs a new kitchen, bathroom, boiler, plastering, fully painting, new carpets, front door replacement and a perimeter fence. My estimation is that this would cost somewhere in the region of £12,000 to complete, now without fee's, SDLT, utilities, mortgage and council tax payments during the renovation process the property stands at £77,000. There is fair to a good chance that after renovation this property is only worth somewhere in the region of £85,000 due to the increasing hardship of

finding suitable BMV properties, yet you are the one who has had to endure the arduous renovation process.

Either organising un-organisable, unreliable and incompetent tradesmen or working your fingers to the bone by renovating yourself.

Now you have to ask yourself a very simple question at the end of all this, would it be better to have the £3,000-£8,000 in equity in the property or would it have been better or easier just to buy the £85,000 property down the road that is already fully renovated.

One way of looking at this is, what if after this period of renovation the property market has declined a few percent and your equity is now absorbed by this decline? And If the market increases over this period, then you have equity anyway. Whatever the value of equity means when you don't plan to sell is a different story altogether.

Now, if your strategy is to buy, renovate, release maximum equity, then it's the prior of the two regardless of the endurance.

Although if that is your strategy, you would probably not have bought that particular property as the maths doesn't really stack up in the case of the 'releasing equity model'.

Ok, so why the pessimistic view on the revaluation, I thought there was a lot of money in renovating property?

Well, you might not personally know, since you may not move in this circle, many investors but believe me when you start talking and start living this game you will realise that there are lots and lots of part time, full time and potential investors all looking for that elusive £65,000 property.

They are all hoping that after their £12,000 investment the property is going to be worth £100,000, this creates demand and competition thus reducing your chances of finding let alone completing on a property of such sorts but also driving up the price of the £65,000 to £100,000 potential to somewhere nearer £80,000 purchase price.

This is not to say it doesn't happen anymore of course, but it is far harder than it used to be, and it is getting harder as the years roll by to acquire such properties.

Demand for rental property is probably at an all-time high, and the estate agents know this, this is why half of the properties on Rightmove under £100,000 often say IDEAL INVESTMENT OPPORTUNITY as opposed to ideal first time buy, as if we need to be told what a good investment property is.

I wouldn't say the days are gone, but certainly gone are the easy days of finding a property, spending £10,000 and profiting a further £20,000, searching for these properties now is a skill set and with the rise of property sourcing companies and auction houses, it's getting harder and harder.

For my second example let us assume that your strategy is to invest your savings initially and then couple further savings with the return on the investment or your cash flowing property, we will use our maths to demonstrate the difference between refurbishing and buying either complete or in a good rentable condition.

Once again, we will, for the purposes of demonstration minus all associated costs including SDLT, they are somewhat relative to the two demonstrations anyway.

We purchase the property as in the example above for £65,000, 75% leveraged from the lender and 25% from our savings.

That means we put down £16,250 and spend a further £12,000 on renovating the property bringing our total investment to £28,250. This also excludes all the mortgage and council tax payments due to lost rent while renovating over let's say a three month period, not to mention the manually removed hair and fingernails, although they will grow back.

The nails definitely

The alternative here is to go ahead and buy the £85,000 property that's already to rent, either renovated by someone else or maybe it's a good condition family home that will let no problem without any further investment.

Again using a 75% leveraged loan and 25% from our savings. Our contribution would be £21,250 in order to complete.

The property is ready to rent immediately with no hassles of renovating or refurbishing further without paying any unnecessary council tax, energy bills or factoring in lost rent.

We have an extra £7,000 in the bank towards our next investment, and with the high cash flowing rent coming in approximately 3-4 months beforehand we will get to our next £20,000 target a whole lot faster, more than a year faster in fact. This, in turn, enables us to buy our next property more than 14 months quicker which means we then have the revenue coming in from two properties for 12-14 months longer which means that our growth in this instance over the renovating strategy will grow exponentially faster the longer we adopt this.

For those of you who like hard figures, I will demonstrate the mathematics loosely here:

The property rents for £500, the interest-only mortgage repayments are £122 (rounded up) as you borrowed £48,750 on a 3% product, so your Cashflow is £328/month.

Assuming all best-case scenarios and a self-managed property your yearly accrued pre-tax profit would be £4,536 meaning it would take around 4.4 years to achieve your next target of £20,000 without external investment.

This is if you relied solely on your investment income, which in itself is ok, it's definitely better than what your initial invested capital would achieve devaluing in the bank over the 4.4 years.

However, in the second strategy, we are up £7,000 because we haven't had to inject a lump sum to renovate the property.
We are still on an interest only mortgage, but our payments are slightly higher since we leveraged 75% of £85,000 this time. This means based on the same mortgage product our repayment is £160 (rounded up) meaning our yearly pre-tax profit is £4,080 which when added to the £7,000 we retained by investing in a ready to rent property means it takes us approximately 3.2 years to acquire our next £20,000 investment sum without external investment.

We now, for the next 12-14 months depending on how quickly we act, have £8,160 coming in as opposed to £4,536 in cash flow getting us closer to our next goal even faster as a result.
Now as I explained, if you were to continue down each particular strategy exclusively in a parallel universe the growth on strategy two would increase exponentially faster than in strategy one.
A quick side note, if you are unfamiliar with the term exponential then take a small break and google the term, understanding this is crucial if you want to be a professional investor, there are many great articles, charts and videos you can watch.

The above example is not here to convince you that buying properties ready to rent is the right way to go about your business, and I certainly do not discredit the renovation route either, both avenues are within my strategy and frequently adopted.

The reason for the demonstration is to highlight that there are choices to be made and it would always be wise to remain open-minded on each and every property treating them with individual merit.

But also to open your mind further than that of what has been drummed into you by TV programs or unqualified assumptions of misinformed individuals.

We are all aware through passive comments that its great to buy low, renovate and reap the rewards.

I have conversation after conversation with people who ask me that very question at a party or dinner when I mention that I am a property investor. The returned statement is usually, "what do you buy cheap to renovate and then sell them on".

As if it was as simple as that, its just misconception.

The problem is it gets ingrained into your subconscious, so my job here is to demonstrate other avenues that exist and prove their credibility with mathematics.

Incidentally and by no means of a so-called better strategy, I do tend to buy more properties these days that do not need renovating and are 'ready to go', but that is mainly because I do not need the equity to remortgage in order to acquire further funds.

Also, I simply got fed up of renovating properties myself or paying tradesmen to do work on a property that in essence and given time I could have done myself, even in my 'new world' way of thinking that is hard to swallow.

As a contrast, the last three single let properties and the last HMO I acquired, two had To-Let boards up one week before we completed this is because they are what I call 'turnkey properties.

One property needed about £1,500 spending on it, mainly a couple of carpets, a dab of paint and the old fire removing which took only ten days or so. The other was a complete renovation top to bottom which took around eight weeks.

These are all genuine buys which accurately reflect and demonstrate my varied strategy.

The two properties that had the To-Let boards up one week prior to completion were purchased for about the current market value, perhaps £3,000-£5,000 under but that did reflect in the fact that in the coming years perhaps 4-6 they are going to need some kind of modernisation.

The other was about £8,000 under the current market value but really could have done with a new bathroom immediately, and there were some other older features that I chose not to modernise due to the request to rent speedily by an elderly lady.

The final property, the one that needs fully renovating will need a good £35,000 spending on it but we will re-finance this at a stupidly high rate, releasing all our money from the deal plus a good deal of extra revenue to start the process all over again. This property is an HMO and can be refinanced as a business taking the yearly rental income and multiplying it by approximately 6-10 times, depending on where you are in the country. We are renovating this property significantly by converting it from a four bedroom townhouse into a six bed HMO. This is a whole different story and ball game altogether.

The examples above are used to illustrate that your strategy doesn't have to be one track minded and that providing the maths stack up then so does the deal, providing, of course, all other factors are satisfactory, location etc.

If I were to continue or slightly change the earlier example to show that once the property was renovated, it would be worth £95,000 then it is an entirely different story.

Putting £28,250 into buying and renovating would be a superior choice especially if your strategy was Cashflow since the revaluation and subsequent re-mortgage of the property would free up £71,250. Meaning you could pay back your initial mortgage of £48,750 leaving you with £22,500 in your pocket. The result is that you only have £5,750 left in the deal giving you, a quickly worked out return on investment of 82%. Yes that's pretty high, pretty desirable and none of your friends or anyone you meet at networking events will believe you, and if they do, stick with them, get to know them, befriend them, work with them because they understand the industry and more importantly the laws of money.

The above illustration was worked out excluding fees and costs, based on a £600 per month rental income over a 25-year interest only loan at approximately 3.5%, with the exception of the exclusion of fees this is all highly achievable.

In summary to part 1 and to draw a conclusion, hopefully, I have shown you good examples and helped you to understand some of the different aspects of the many different strategies available to each and every one of us.

Remember no two strategies will ever be the same, maybe in principle but not in detail.
Not only are strategies so different in terms of the way they are implemented but also fabricated.
The fundamentals in your strategy might be the same as a close colleagues, but the way you implement them may be of polar opposites due to your understanding of the principles or the fears and desires you both hold.

In short, talk to people whom you admire, wish to emulate or who have traits that you do not. Don't be single-minded about your strategy unless your finances or fears dictate this and, in the latter, try to overcome this through the power of adopting positive thoughts and continued education. Think carefully about your overall aim, your personality and bear in mind your financial situation always when choosing your mortgage type.

Before you even understand the property market, you must get to grips with the mathematical equations that will help you drive your strategy faster and with far less risk or work.

Understanding the maths is the most important thing, get that wrong, and you could be heading for a world of pain. You do not necessarily have to be amazing at maths, however.

I am sat here writing this book with a Casio MX-8V calculator to my right and a spreadsheet open on my second monitor to the left.

Both are used not just as a reference or as confirmation but because I failed GSCE mathematics miserably.

I have read dozens of books on property investing and on business success in general and it is a common theme that the author is not only far from being a mathematical genius but rather quite poor at maths in general, as well as other forms of academia.

Great, it makes me feel at ease and like I explained before on my rather harsh rant, if it's not a quality you possess either make it a quality or seek the advice and guidance of another more qualified individual.

You do not need to be rain-man, nor do you need a degree in mathematics, but you do need to understand the mathematical equations even if that is just so that you can transport them to a spreadsheet.

I have developed many simple spreadsheets from my initially limited knowledge of Excel, ones on which I can alter individual cells to give desired results; this is how I overcame my poor maths skills initially. Admittedly the more I learn, and the more I use, the better I get, and that will be the same for all of you.

If your reading this with a comprehensive understanding of the workings of Sir Isaac Newton having just read the Principia Mathematica in its original Latin then great you are already ahead of most of the investors I know, in fact, if it's the latter then you're definitely ahead of any property investor I know, and perhaps property isn't the best way for you to make your millions.

I am sure that there are many other determining factors that I have not talked about yet that will help each and every one of you come to understand your strategy or at least your initial strategy.

Hopefully, the above-discussed topics have given you enough underpinning knowledge so that you can have somewhat of a head start in figuring this all out.

I would stress the importance of having a clear and tailored strategy unique to your own individual needs and desires. However, if one single factor like mathematics is stopping you from investing then maybe it would be beneficial letting your experience aid you in developing a strategy based on the rest of your strengths and using leverage to help with the maths.

After all, it is far more important that you act rather than letting anything get in the way. If you wait until your strategy is perfected, you'll be waiting forever. A good strategy is one that continually evolves.

What is right for you, in the beginning, may not be what is right for you in five years' time.

Markets change, trends change and your strategy needs to change to mirror these.

After all in five years' time, you will be in a whole different position than you are now and your strategy will or at least should reflect that.

Part 2 - Purchasing Property
Chapter 1, Finding Suitable Properties

Ok, so part 1 of the book 'getting started' is now done and dusted.

We are swiftly moving on to the nuts and bolts of the industry.
In this part, part 2, I intend on walking you through the sourcing and viewing processes as well as discussing offering and negotiations.
I will then demonstrate the purchasing process from the offer being accepted by the vendor to the collection of the keys from the agent.

I intend to fulfil my promise and include a clear and far more accurate overview of all the costs associated with buying a property.
Up to now all of my examples have been rough costings in which I have purposely excluded the associated fees.
As I have previously mentioned this was not an attempt to sugar coat the profits or to gloss over the fact that there are all sorts of
"Oh, Id like a piece of that" fees put on by lenders to squeeze you out of every ounce of your hard earned profits, but rather for the purpose of quick and easy demonstration.

This is now perhaps a convenient place to mention the withdrawal of tax relief for owners of second homes or investment properties that used to give us landlords as well as first-time buyers 0% stamp duty to pay on properties under £125,000.

In April 2016, in their attempts to raise extra revenue from the likes of you and I, the government introduced a 3% surcharge on SDLT for anyone who owns a second home, being an investment property or a holiday home.

This 3% charge is now, for most investors the biggest factor associated with the purchase fees (outside of the mortgage contribution of course) and something that you all must factor into your initial calculations or business plan.

Along with the addition of the 3% SDLT, there is now an incremental elimination of interest payments being used to offset profits against tax at the 40% rate for higher rate taxpayers, but I will speak about this in depth later in the book in the 'Personal V's Company' chapter.

Early on in part 1, I showed you the various means of sourcing property and gave you a brief description as well as my opinions on each method. As all the information given to this point can be somewhat overwhelming and may seem like an age ago here is a quick recap of the list.

1) The newspaper
2) The estate agent, their window, website and phone-line
3) The internet – sites like Rightmove, Zoopla, YOURMOVE, On The Market and Prime Location
4) Property auctions
5) Professional property sourcing companies

6) Facebook
7) Friends, family, work colleagues or clients
8) Landlords associations
9) Leaflet distribution
10) For sale boards

The list has some excellent avenues, some not so excellent avenues and some that are quite frankly a waste of resources.

From here on in let us assume that, unless otherwise stated I am talking about Rightmove as the primary avenue, it is, in my opinion, the best online medium to find property, all the above methods for sourcing including all other online portals have their individual differences, pros and cons but I simply prefer Rightmove.

I explained earlier about the importance of establishing a good relationship with the local estate agents; this is something that is very important not only when viewing and offering on property but in terms of gathering information also.

A good relationship with a local estate agent can prove invaluable when you need questions answering that your research simply can't give you.

Having a solid relationship means they will be more likely to provide you with the privileged information that they maybe shouldn't or wouldn't if your relationship wasn't as established.

If your relationship **has** been cemented in the way I advise then this information can be a major point score if you can get it.

Along with the cash potential of the property, having the agent like you and feel valued by you is one of your highest concerns when viewing any property, everything else is secondary for the time being. You will after reading this section have a firmer understanding of what to look for on your viewings. You will become after so many viewings, an expert on what to look out for, how to spot or how to quickly determine a properties potential.

This is all experience gathering, and the following pages will help you with this, but you must ensure from day one that the agent understands that you are a genuine buyer and that you are a likeable, honest and reliable person who intends to make his or her life that little bit easier given a chance. Only then will the estate agent start to work for you, which is the desired end result.

When you have established your investment area, and when you have determined your budget, overall or general strategy based on goals and circumstance it is time to start getting stuck in. It is time to begin viewing property, for me the real excitement begins here, the formalities have been undertaken, and the reality is now setting in. The skills needed to progress change somewhat here, the mathematics are predetermined the goals are set, and the laptop gets closed.

The ideas swirling around your head like the storm raging within Jupiters red spot should now be controlled and implemented carefully. Your vision, awareness and research now take precedence over all of your careful planning.

With so many readers having so many different varied strategies I can't possible exemplify them all, I will, however, demonstrate what I did in the beginning and generally still do now when looking for a suitable property.
Viewing property personally is something I still do myself on a weekly basis.

I do have colleagues and know of other professional investors that have a nominated person or a team sourcing and even viewing properties on their behalf, but to be honest, I love it. It's the one thing within the industry that still really excites me.
I like nothing better than spotting a bargain, a property with potential or a great cash flow opportunity. I love picking up on things others can't see, I love walking into a property and knowing within few short minutes if this is going to be the next addition to my portfolio or if in fact we are done with the viewing.

I have developed such personal relationships with some of the agents in my area over the last ten years that I can quite literally walk into a property and within 2 minutes tell them that we are done here and that this is not for me and they completely understand this.

They know my experience and respect that I won't waste anyone's time, but they also know that after 2-3 minutes I am often saying "ok I'll have this one here is my offer", no messing and its concrete so we have a mutual understanding.

For me, this is the thrill of the industry, along with the cash flow and exponential growth of course.

Before I demonstrate my approach, I want to discuss a few things that may be relevant to you, how to spot them and some ways of improving your searches.

When looking at properties look for clues that tick the boxes set out within your criteria or strategy. For example, if you want property to refurbish or renovate then look out for listings showing pictures of the front of the property only. Look for tape over the toilet seat, across the taps, on the oven and gas appliances. This tape is 'do not use' or 'decommissioned' tape which, like the latter suggests, all the appliances have been decommissioned which is common practice in repossessions. Look for properties that are empty inside showing immediate vacancies these show that the owner has already moved on to another property or in fact another life.

These properties may be acquired cheaper as the owners are often losing money through mortgage, council tax, insurance, and utility payments.

Along with the pictures in the listing look at the wording within the description, that give clues.

Words like IMMEDIATE POSSESSION or NO CHAIN also may suggest that either the property is a repossessed home, is a deceased estate or the vendor has moved into his newly fancy built plasterboard property. Again these signs may point towards being able to purchase the property cheaper and simpler than you would have to otherwise.

If you want a good solid property as a long-term retirement plan or a lower risk type of investment then maybe you want a property that has been looked after lovingly and improved somewhat over the years by a careful owner, and you don't mind paying that little bit extra to achieve this.

If this is the case look for signs that demonstrate the owners care for the property like the condition of the garden. Is it tidy, well kept and presented? This has always been a real clue to me that the property has been taken care of. Look for newly finished or fully fitted bathrooms and kitchens with good clean appliances or fixtures. Again this shows the vendor has not scrimped on the fundamentals or saved on the major overheads of a home. Nice front doors, as well as well-painted fences and clean newer eaves and guttering, also show that the vendor cares about the aesthetics of the property. If they care what it looks like from the outside, there is a better than average chance they have taken good care of it internally.

We will talk more about the internals of the property later on in the viewing chapter.

Word of caution; I generally look out for and for the best part stay clear of, properties that show an internal picture as its main listings image. This, to me, screams 'bad area'. The general protocol is for an agent to show the front elevation of the property on the listing page and the internals secondary. Listings that show a living room rather than a well presented front elevation just put me off. Why not place the properties frontal on the listing like everyone else, is my first question, and there is, for the best part, usually a wrong answer that follows.

Remember that the curb appeal of the property is something that will also put potential tenants off.

This general approach of listing the front elevation may change over time, but until it does, and agents start listing the best feature of the property primarily, then I will stick by this judgment.

As previously mentioned, I use all of, or at least most of Rightmove's abundant features, but I also use spreadsheets to analyse and more specifically, categorise properties.

I have a varied and detailed strategy specific to my different business being the personal approach (which incidentally is now dormant as it is at capacity), my investment company, the HMO or commercial company etc.

As a general rule, however, I mainly buy three types of single let property through Wise Owl which is the management company. Although, as I write this book, I am mainly buying one type of single let property specifically. Over the years this has varied relative to circumstance, and as I am always open to new ideas and strategy changes, so I will summarise all three for you.

I like to have my researched properties filed according to these three types, Rightmove can't really do this for me so after I have had results filtered in the second stage of research for me by my staff, I then use my spreadsheets for further analysis.

The first type of property I buy or used to buy was the good old fixer-upper.

This is something I think most landlords have started out in the interim doing. This method did prove very successful for me, especially in the early years and especially since I was relatively DIY minded and therefore could keep costs down by doing the bulk of the work myself. I remember those days, working all the hours that god sent striping woodchip and sanding doorframes to save a few hundred quid, what on earth was I thinking?

It wasn't all that bad I suppose it did teach me the value of my time and also how long specific jobs take which meant I was clued up later on in life when builders tried to tell me about the extremities of the job. I usually just smile politely now knowing what I have learned from these lessons.

It did also mean however that over ten years later in the here, and now after just selling a few of these properties to one of my investment companies, it helped to make quite a tidy little sum since the properties were very cheap to purchase due to the work required. Now years later with some capital growth coupled with my incredibly low cost but fantastic improvements they are worth a lot more, yielding a greater profit for me.

Money to spend on a boat perhaps, a fancy car or a luxury holiday I hear you ask? Not on your life! Money to invest in property I hear you sigh... Or maybe that was my wife.

Although I am now editing this book in a private villa in Bordeaux while my kids are splashing around in the heated pool, and my wife is chilling a bottle of Pouilly fuisse to go with our evening meal it's not all work work work, there has to be a balance and an ultimate or definite aim. This has to be a lifestyle, not a job, but I've touched on that already and will keep drumming it home throughout. I may be on holiday, but I still have work to do, ok maybe it is all work work work, I'll get back to you on that one!

Ok, so the second type of property I buy are three bedroom townhouses or ex-council that require only a small amount of investment to make them rentable. This is an approximate investment of between £500 and £3,000. These are between £65,000 and £85,000 although this figure sometimes gets distorted when a circumstantial property becomes available. Maybe the property is a little cheaper than this, but I know the tenants are very good, long-term settled tenants since I've managed this property for a few years or maybe it's a little more expensive, but again the circumstances make it a good buy like the location is very desirable, thus yielding a great rental price.

Rent here in my area of the North East is relatively good in comparison to purchase price. I live in a small town between a couple of larger towns, but funnily enough, the properties that meet this criterion, 3 bedrooms, mid terraced properties with small to medium gardens tend to come in at roughly the same price as the larger towns.
The rentals here, in my opinion, are far better, however.
They have fewer reoccurring issues and yield a better overall return on my capital due to the reduced competition and general longer sustaining tenants.

A three-bedroom property in my local town purchased around the £65,000 mark can rent from £450-£495 and can increase to over £550 when spending somewhere in the region of £85,000.
With an interest only, buy to let mortgage in a personal portfolio (personal because the mortgage rates are generally lower) that's a return on investment of between 18% and 21%.
do you see why I like my local area so much?

This figure can be achieved in the surrounding larger towns, but like I say the competition is stronger and to achieve it the hassle factor increases somewhat. We spend far too much time sorting these kinds of hassles out for other landlords for me not to observe, take note, learn and implement a change in plan.

The third type of property I buy falls into the random pile, something I see that I just think stacks up for a particular reason. This is where experience really comes into play, and it is what separates professional investors form the older type landlord pile.
It's where savvy or imaginative investors can excel, and this is not something you can be taught in any book or classroom.
I buy these for so many varied reasons.
Maybe it's in an area that I am familiar with the rental demand due to my letting business, and it's cheap because it's a repossession needing work.

Maybe it's a two bedroom, not something I want to buy many of, although because of stock levels I have been recently, but it is in a good area where rent is high, or it's a little over what I would usually pay but has a decent re-mortgage potential due to the area, or it is a quick sale property like a deceased estate or the seller has bought a new build, and the building company is selling on their behalf etc.

Whatever the reason is, the fact is that the property falls outside of my usual criteria, but I am more than willing to adapt to suit, providing I think it stacks up well.

Although your requirements will perhaps differ here and the price of property in your area may be vastly different the fundamentals are predominantly the same, so how I go about finding these three types of property is as follows:

I will, since my price range is roughly £65k-£85k head to Rightmove and after indicating the chosen area, select the no-minimum price setting and set the maximum to £90k. Sometimes I will look at 100k, but generally, they will go onto the random spreadsheet. I always set the bedrooms at two for the minimum with No maximum.

As I have explained I tend not to buy two bedroom properties, but I have been changing my strategy lately, and I want to be fully aware of the price comparison between the two along with the demand in case it flips the ROI in favour of the two bedrooms significantly.

The only two bedroom properties I have previously bought within my personal portfolio, like the one I have very recently completed on, were either introduced to me by an agent as a good quick sale or by clients wanting to sell up.

The ROI is not the primary factor here for me, it's the turnaround in tenants due to expanding families, this is why I generally stay clear, although like I mentioned I am always open to change.

All the other main features on Rightmove are set at the defaults. Here is where I will start to scan the properties slowly setting the 'sort' button so that the properties ascend from the lowest price initially.
I scan the page and literally anything I see that catches my eye for whatever reason, even if initially it just ticks one of my boxes gets the little love heart to the right checked and therefore added to my 'Saved Properties' within 'My Rightmove'.
The next job is to filter through the saved properties in 'My Rightmove'.

These now get my full and undivided attention. I had Property Bee loaded onto my browser permanently so I could see the listings history immediately, but now I have to do this through property tracker as I explained earlier in the book.
I can now fully assess each property individually to see if any of them actually do meet my criteria. If so they get saved and if not they get deleted. I am usually left with around six or seven properties at the end of this process.

I now transfer the data from these properties to the appropriate spreadsheet. The first tab on the spreadsheet is tilted 'rentable'; this generally means that it is either rentable in its current condition or it will be with a small investment of £3,000 or less. The second is titled investment; this means that under no circumstances would I rent this property in its present state or that it needs either a general refurbishment or a full renovation to bring it up to my specific and ever-evolving standard.

The third tab on the bottom of the spreadsheet is aptly titled random, and this really is self-explanatory thus needs no expansion.

So, the above search of Rightmove may not surprise you or even teach you anything that you didn't already know, but the next step is where I feel it gets efficient and what tends to separate my research form that of others, especially that of part-time investors.

As well as having a great eye for potential and an excellent idea of generally what works and what doesn't in the industry I am also, like many other successful entrepreneurs, a spreadsheet nerd. I will gladly spend hours in front of the PC with a good spreadsheet loaded, looking at variable outcomes, there is nothing better than looking at figures when they affirm your initial assumptions or demonstrate favourable outcomes mathematically.

I will manually input all the data from these properties into my spreadsheet individually, starting with the listed value, moving through to the achievable rent.
I list the SDLT fees, solicitors fees, projected refurbishment, renovation or sprucing costs, amount of leveraged capital, mortgage repayments based on the interest rates from my last few mortgages

until I have my monthly Cashflow and subsequently the ROI results in the end columns.

I have an identical sheet just below this where I can take the results and play with them slightly by altering the rental income based on the internals or overall desirability of the property.

Aesthetics, bedroom size, storage space, gardens, driveways can all increase the rental income, so I adjust accordingly.
I alter the list price to a more realistic sale price and recheck the ROI's. This is based somewhat on experience but can just as easily be based on recent sold history or comps as it's known, not to mention talking with the agent as by now you will have developed a great relationship.

You can also determine this price by merely inputting what you are prepared to pay for the property. With a small amount of research, you can gauge somewhat what my experience tells me initially and input the results accordingly.
looking through these results, I will approach the agents to view in accordance with the most potential or greatest ROI result.
This method reduces my time wasted on viewings while increasing my cash flow or returns to the maximum possible outcome and over the course of my portfolio a few percent here and there has the potential to yield much higher results.

If I had adopted this philosophy from day one, I would have achieved my current status long before now and potentially relieved myself of some of the unwanted earlier properties.

I will do this individually for tab 1, rentable, but tab 2, investment is a little more complicated as I need factor in a re-mortgage value and also need to quite accurately evaluate the amount required as a cash investment to bring the property up to a good standard in order to re-mortgage and therefore release funds to either release my initial investment or to have as little money left in the deal as is reasonably possible, if this is my desire.

This, unfortunately, is something only experience can tell you, but the sheet can still be produced after viewing the property if this is your approach and in time it will get more and more accurate.

Tab 3 is as random as the tab itself, but generally, the procedure of analysis from tab 1 or tab 2 can be implemented based on what the property requires.

You can see the idea with the spreadsheets, and you could devise your own easily, determined by your own specific strategy.

These sheets are a great way to maximise profit, so they work for any type of investor from the single purchase 'retirement fund' type investor right through to the taking over the world type of investor, after all, we all want the maximum profit from our investments and maximum return from our hard earned cash regardless, this is ultimately why we do what we do and one of the main reasons we've chosen property to achieve it.

These spreadsheets and their uses are demonstrated in depth on our property training courses, and all who attend will get the sheets and formulas to use at their convenience at home. They are incredibly simple to use, by merely adjusting the indicated cells to reflect your figures, everything else is auto calculated and demonstrated for you. To find out more about our courses, please visit www.wiseowlpropertytraining.co.uk

Remember only you truly know your strategy and criteria for an individual property so never let the agent or anyone else, with the exception of a paid, trusted and most importantly experienced advisers talk you into buying a property that goes against your strategy. These paid advisers are the only people that should have your genuine interest at heart.

Remember that properties do come and go on an ever revolving carousel of bricks and mortar. Sometimes I fire Rightmove up and think, 'wow there is nothing on the market at the moment' then three weeks later it's 'wow where have I been the last few weeks'. The best thing about Rightmove and perhaps my favourite time-saving feature as I've mentioned is that of the periodic search.

After you've done the initial sorting and saving of listings, you can then search periodically through the 'added in the last 24hrs, last 7 days, last 14 days feature. You can save your periodic search to fit in with your schedule and only be presented with the newest properties. You can also get instant notifications on listings that match your search criteria as soon as they are uploaded by the agent but as I will explain in a short while, tread lightly here.

Evaluating your findings. So, you've found some properties that seem to tick all your boxes, you really like the look of them, and they seem to be a perfect fit for your chosen strategy. You've added the data to your spreadsheets and have one that comes out on top with a desirable ROI and cash flow. You must now look at the comparables to ensure that this property really is the one.

By the comparables, I mean the other properties that are for sale in the area.

After all, you do not want to buy the most expensive property on the street just because the kitchen is new and it has the greenest grass. Conversely, you may not want to buy the cheapest property on the street because the kitchen is old, and the grass is brown and overgrown.

The kitchen may be extensive, have no gas supply or radiators present and prove to be too big of a cost to renovate economically. Likewise, the garden might have no access to the back deeming it necessary to skip everything by carting it through the property in an L shape fashion, through the kitchen and over the carpet that you did not really want to replace if possible. This may damage the walls you did not want to skim and all to save 5k on a purchase price which on reflection only costs around £1,400 extra in your deposit contribution and SDLT.

The other fundamental approach when looking at the comparables is to look at the sold prices in the street or local streets and to compare this to the market trends of the date sold.

For example, it's all very well buying a property for £100,000 if the others in the street sold for £100,000 or above but if the market has declined recently or the comparables were sold some five years ago for £100,000 in a very strong market, then the figure quoted may not reflect this property's true market value at present. Sometimes agents do try to correct trends or can be a little too late to adjust their stock to reflect the current trend or even have very argumentative or stubborn vendors reluctant to accept a downward trend.

Use due diligence, be patient and take time to complete your research thoroughly.

So how do you determine if the property is of good value, I hear you call?

Ok, let us say that you have found a property in your chosen area.

It's for sale for £75,000. A three-bedroom mid-terrace property in an ex-council area of a small town, funnily enough almost identical to the ones I invest in. Great, good choice this will make it a lot easier for me to explain.

So how do I, I mean you determine if this is a good buy or even an accurate reflection of its current market value. Well the process I go through is this: Firstly I will flick through the photos online, does it need refurbishment or renovation. If so is that my current strategy, I have already suggested that my strategy changes from property to property and over time but is this your strategy at the present time or fundamentally. If so continue, if not carry on looking at the different listings. If you're open to either, then carry on using this process.

Let's determine how much the property needs in order to bring it up to the standard required for the rental market. The pictures should give a good understanding of this.

Are there limited pictures, none of say the kitchen or bathroom? If this is the case, it would be safe to assume that these rooms need a complete overhaul, after all, if the kitchen or bathroom is perfectly adequate why the agent or vendor would omit them from the listing is anyone's guess? If the only picture is of the property itself but none of the interior it is safe to assume that the entire property needs renovating, and this is the consensus going forward, are you ready for this? Are you capable of this? Does your budget stretch to this? These are the questions that should already have been answered in planning your strategy, but they may need revisiting at this stage.

Let's assume that every room in the property has a picture and you can determine the amount of work that is necessary, in your opinion to get this property to your desired rentable state. The next thing to do would be to judge a time frame for the work required. if it's a quick paint and carpet job it is going to take no time at all but if the kitchen needs replacing along with the boiler and bathroom, there is woodchip on the wall, and the windows are single glazed it probably won't surprise you to hear that this is going to take somewhat longer.

Look at the implications of this timeframe, do you need to take this hassle on or will you, by taking this on yield greater returns. In order to determine this, you will need to look at the recently sold history feature on Rightmove. If the other properties in that street are selling for £100,000-£111,000 and you have estimated the work would come in at around £15,000 then I would advise booking a viewing, remember this property is for sale for £75,000. If the work was insurmountable, and the prices in the street were averaging £85,000-£95,000 then I personally, would again consider booking a viewing, after all my strategy may be different to yours altogether, and although historically I did, at the moment I am not overly interested in obtaining my properties well under the current market value for a refurb and re-mortgage strategy.

I am much more concerned with cash flow at the minute while the interest rates are so low and money is so cheap to leverage. There also comes a point in your business or plan when just paying current market value for a property that I don't intend on selling for 25 years and having it in my portfolio working for me immediately beats waiting around to buy a property for a few grand under the current market value. I will put emphasis here on the word current; market values are continually changing, remember that the next time someone offers you a 'Below Market Value' or BMV property.

Paying the current market value for a property may not be an aggressive growth strategy or the best way to get the most from your initial capital pot but it saves messing around with tradesmen, renovating over a period, organising kitchen designers, plumbers, builders or rubbish removals and then dealing with brokers, mortgage companies and valuers to release the capital that at the moment I do not necessarily need or desire. If capital is limited then you need to look closer at this, but if you have enough for compounding and exponential growth to set in then it may be a great lower hassle approach, again this all comes down to your strategy plan initially and why we all have a different strategy.

If the property in the same area has been selling recently and by recently I mean in the same economic climate, for around £95,000 and the work to renovate is £15,000, then I would disregard the property as it's not really worth the time and hassle to renovate in order to save a few grand. It may be insurmountable in terms of the deposit required to purchase a similar property two doors up that has been fully modernised. We would be paying an extra 5k on top of our 25% contribution but saving 10k on the renovation fee, thus leaving a surplus of funds in our pocket and without the hassle factor and timeframe associated.

Once I have a property that interests me I will do some research on the area itself. As this property is in your local area or chosen area and by the best part you will have some sort of idea of the streets/areas within, this research starts by looking at the map feature on Rightmove to gain confirmation of the general area of the town, village or city in which this particular street falls. This will also show the surrounding areas or streets if you're not too familiar with the street itself.

The next thing to do is a couple of drive-bys on the property; Now I am not advocating any sort of gangland-style violence hear but rather a quiet, no harm intended pass of the property in my un-pimped up car at various times of the day to establish certain factors.
Perhaps consider one during 8-9am to see the extent of the 'school run' or work traffic. Maybe one at midday to get an idea of the local residents who may be coming or going through the daytime and one around tea time after things are settled. If I end up considering offering on the property, I will do a few more at various times or days, sometimes just when I'm passing or visiting a nearby property.

These drive-bys give a great insight to the goings on of the property; it gives you an understanding of the local residents, the parking availability or restrictions that there may be as well as the overall feeling of the street.
If everything seems ok, then it helps stack the chips in the 'decent purchase' camp.

One point worth mentioning here is that I always try to carry out these drive-bys in dry conditions, and preferably, season depending when the sun is out. It gives a clearer indication as people are just more active in the sun, especially through the day. You'll see a lot more sofas out in front of the houses from the congregations in the sunshine.

In summary: If the property is for sale at a different price to others in the street but you can see a specific reason why it's either a few thousand more, like if the property has a garage or a conservatory, or it is vastly cheaper as it needs a full renovation and you feel the work inputted would yield the desired outcome or justify the project then its probably at the right price.
If it's at around the same price as the recent sold prices or there is an explainable reason why this differs and if you deem the area to be desirable, not overpopulated with to-let boards and of sound construction, then the property is also for sale at the right price. The next stage is to view the property internally and determine if the photos do it justice or instead flatter the agent's photographer.

Part 2 - Purchasing Property

Chapter 2, Contacting the Agents and Viewing the Property

You have completed your research fully and looked at the properties in your saved searches on Rightmove to determine the best ROI property or the properties that best suit your chosen strategy with the help of your spreadsheets. You've carried out your, no harm intended drive-bys and your careful analysis of the comparables gives you the confidence that up to this point everything stacks up. It's now time to approach the agents for the viewings.

You may think this is a straightforward process or call to action; anyone can use a phone or send a viewing request through Rightmove, right? Well, you'd be right for the best part but completely wrong for the rest of it.

Yes anyone can carry out the above actions but you've probably got many properties saved within your spreadsheets ready to view, and this is great it will give you, hopefully, diversity and choice.
It means that you get the property you want, it means that you get it at the price you know is right for you and your strategy and you get to choose the best one from a pile of say 10 prospective properties. There are however a few too many scenarios the contain the word you in the last few sentences.

There are others involved in the equation here, one being the agent, the agent that you want to, fundamentally, no matter what, build and or maintain a good and positive, mutually beneficial relationship with. The agent who you want to show how serious you are about this whole investment game.

You certainly don't want the agent to believe your window shopping or viewing everything and anything until you perhaps may eventually decide to offer on maybe one of the properties providing its perfect. You don't want the agent to think their time is not valued or even worse, is wasted, this is not an effective way to forge long-lasting and strong relations.

Some might say so what, it's their job to show you the properties, it's what they get paid for, it's you who is buying and keeping them in a job. Well although this has a small element of truth, this attitude is one for the rookies, the people who make mistakes. What you have to think about here is the way the agent views you as an investor and as a potential customer. If you ultimately want them to work for you in the long term, then you have to be smart in your approach.

If you intend to solely purchase one or perhaps two properties and possibly some others much further down the line, then act as you will, but if you want to progress and have the intentions or aspirations in becoming a full-time or successful property investor, then please take note of the above and the following text.

My advice here would be, and this is something I practise personally, is to highlight the best properties on the spreadsheet in order of suitability and then bulk them into either weeks or agents.

I never view more than two properties with an agent at the same time. It is fine to call the agent to inform them you've seen two properties that meet your criteria and you would like to view both. This gives them the impression that you've done your research and you'll most likely, providing it all stacks up, have the intentions of offering on one of the properties. We can then discuss the exit strategy and the further viewings thereafter.

I will guarantee that about 90% of the agents that you come across will arrogantly assume that he or she is far more knowledgeable about property than you. I meet agents on a weekly basis who assume they know more about the industry than me, if only they knew I wrote the bloody book on it huh!!

Along with their arrogance comes the opportunity to get smart, and somewhat deceptive.
I am talking little white lie deceptive here not complete fiction.

This is where you get to view all the other properties you liked initially within that agent's stock and still maintain the relationship and even possibly improving it at the same time.

If either of the two properties you've just viewed, for whatever reason do not float your boat then talk to the agent, let them assume they can "educate" you. Let them have your criteria for rentals and subsequently let them tell you about the other properties on the market that fit into the same criteria, leading them to arrange the other viewings that you wanted to arrange initially anyway.
The properties he mentions that you will have already seen on Rightmove but disregarded, tell him "oh yes I've seen that one and I'm not really interested in it", citing your reasons.

The other properties you are interested in that are on your spreadsheet already, well, let him feel he has been the one to bring you the lead. "Oh great that one sounds good, let's go and see that one, what timeslots do you have" and thank him for this insight. Agents are in the business of showing properties but their commodity within this industry is salesmanship, and if they think that the sale of one property is dead in the water you better believe that they will try to sell you another. This all works to your advantage; you get to maintain strong relations with the agent while having him feel that his time is well spent.

He feels valued that he has either had the chance to "educate" you on his stock or he feels good because he's struck a lead for himself and you still get to see the properties you want with him feeling great about it too, who's the winner here? Well in essence everyone, but mainly you, you would have viewed the property anyway.

The underlining point here is, yes you can still view quite a few properties in one week providing they are for sale with multiple agents, but if there are a few for sale with one particular agent then let them arrange the viewings for you.

Arrange two yourself, and the rest will come as a by-product of those viewings. It may be a slightly slower process but one that will eventually pay dividends so be patient and understand that it is not a race to buy and that stock comes along all the time.

One quick point here, one that ties in nicely with the first point and with the whole agent relationship theme. You must in the first instance, call the agent or better still call in to see the agent with the two properties that you want to view. In today's age of 'anti-social' media, no solid relations are formed in text format whether that being through their Facebook page, their website or by using email, even if that is their preferred method. You will always be a number or a piece of text if you start this way, it is a far quicker route to developing a personal relationship by calling or calling-in to initiate communication than it is any other way, a face to the name is paramount.

You've now contacted the agent using a somewhat clever and prudent thought process, one that is going to maintain or even strengthen the relationship and you've organised a viewing or viewings at a time that suits you.

It is important that you book your viewings at a time that is convenient to your schedule, not theirs. Being tempted to book a viewing at 2:45pm the following day because you either can't wait another 22 hours or as it suits the agent is no good if you need to get the kids from school at 3:15pm. Subsequently rushing your viewing leaving no time to build the rapport and check the necessaries required to determine the properties true value or potential or even to let the agent organise the further viewings of alternative properties.

This will, in turn, be detrimental to the relationship and can give the agent the unwanted opinion that your intentions are not true.

Book an appointment only when you can be certain that you have plenty of time either side of the viewing time slot to allow careful inspection and plentiful conversation and it goes without saying, never cancel a viewing on the same day or even the day before.

Agents tend to have heavily booked diaries with scheduled appointments, so you do not want to be the person to disrupt that, leave that to the unorganised rookie who the agent will never work for.

You should aim to arrive at the property at least 15 minutes before the appointment, but I always get there as early as possible. There are two main reasons I do this, the first is because I want to get a more accurate feel of the area, one that can give you a far better impression than the various drive-bys you've already done, a lot can happen in half an hour and you would be surprised what information you can gather in this time.

The second reason I arrive so early is that, if the agent is good at his job he will no doubt get there early too.

He will want to show you the property in its best possible light, in all its true glory, he will make sure that all the lights are switched on and curtains are open, blinds set at the right height and tilted to allow in maximum light without showing what undesirable features he wants to hide. He will clear the junk mail in front of the door, pick the rubbish up that has blown into the garden and in some cases turn on the heating to give the property a nice warming feel.

He may even turn the extraction on in the kitchen and bathroom to block out the road, street or even noise from the neighbours.

Although the so-called agent's tricks are a representation of the property, it is a representation in a best-case scenario, and that's great you should see that also, you'll be able to see the properties potential. But you also want to see the property in the worst possible light, so you can gauge it accurately.

You can, during the time spent in the car prior to the viewing take a good look at the roofline of the property. Is there a good straight line along the ridge, one that is parallel to the eaves of the property or even in-line with next doors roof. Is it perfectly perpendicular to the end of the property if it's an end terraced, semi-detached or even detached property?

A good straight, parallel to the eaves roofline is especially relevant on a terraced property, look at both neighbouring properties does the line of sight flow or are there dips along the line.
Look at the eaves, are they plastic or wood, what's their overall condition, do they look solid or flimsy, do they look clean or are they rotting and flaky.

The guttering, has this been renewed, are there any signs of leaks at the joints, this will be shown by a green or white colouring on the plastic or down the wall directly under the joint, this is a quick fix if found and repaired early, but left leaking it can, and often does lead to damp in the walls, if the signs of leaking are visible from the road, make a note of the position and check the wall is dry from the inside with a moisture tester, these are very cheap to buy and can save hundreds, sometimes thousands in unexpected damp repairs.

You can look at the condition of the windows, are they clean and are the frames moss or stain free, are the panes misted or starting to fail, beginning to show signs of condensation, this is more prominent or common on south-facing windows due to the increased sun penetration. Do they look like they have been looked after by the vendor this may seem irrelevant or silly to you now, but it will give a good indication of how well the vendor has looked after the property on a whole, if he has not bothered with cleaning the windows it is a safe bet that other aspects of the property will be shown a similar level of neglect.

Take note of the front yard or garden if any, is it in good condition, again just like the windows this can give an indication of the owner's care for the property and its basic maintenance or repair needs.
Is there a fence or wall that encloses the yard or garden, is it a wooden fence, unpainted or untreated and unsecured or is it of brick construction? Are the bricks or coping stones missing or loose, both of these will incur investment and or time and will affect the curb appeal of the property.

Now assess the overall curb appeal of the property, and mark it out of ten. This will be your prospective tenants first impression of the property and often of the area itself, so you want this to be pleasing. After all the tenant for the best part, and if you do your tenant finding correctly, has the choice of where he or she wants to live. Your aim here is to get them to like your property the most out of all they have viewed. As well as marking the initial curb appeal it's worth noting what you think its potential appeal can be with little investment, for instance, is it purely cosmetic and do you think with a brush, power wash and a quick paint you can transform its appeal to achieve a higher score.

Are you surprised what you can determine on a property in a quick ten minutes before a viewing? This is the information that experience gives you, but you can just read my book and gain this knowledge without having to spend many years earning it.

We have, as part of our 101-training programme, a free property checklist for you to download and take with you on viewings to help determine the suitability of the property against your needs.
This will save you time on your viewings and help you to be aware of some things you may have missed or even not know how to check.

So, the agent has arrived and taken you inside, you will either be seeing a property full of furniture as the vendor is still living in his home or more commonly, at least for me over the years, you'll be seeing an empty property.

The latter of the two here is always advantageous since it is very hard to gauge a properties true condition when the vendor has placed his or her furniture very strategically. Pictures over holes or damaged walls, cleaning and scrubbing, spraying air freshener baking fresh loaves of bread in the oven while brewing strong coffee are all common tricks, and seriously these do happen, and more often than you think.

It's perhaps the oldest trick in the book, but it works, who doesn't like the smell of bread baking in an oven or coffee brewing in a pot.

It goes without saying that the overall condition of the property and general feel is of huge importance when deciding to buy a property. Assuming that they are satisfactory, however, to me the main things I look for when viewing a property and this is in no particular order are all compiled below on my anti-superstitious 13 point list:

1) The condition feel and operation of all of the main doors and windows.
2) The condition of carpets and the presence of underlay.
3) The walls, ceilings and their coverings – aertex, woodchip, wallpaper, freshly plastered etc.
4) The condition, standard and age of the kitchen and tiling. The implications of replacing and my best guess to when that would be necessary, and at what cost.
5) The same as above applies to the bathroom.
6) The overall size and layout of the bedrooms but in particular the smallest bedroom.
7) The age and type of central heating system installed.
8) The age and type of consumer unit installed.
9) The size of the gardens, the areas of grassed, paved and fenced parts, and the number of trees or large shrubs.
10) The driveways or parking areas.

11) Roof, fascia's and guttering.

12) Other boards, either To-let or For Sale.

13) Anything else major, noticeable or unusual that jumps out at me.

So that we are on the same page here, I will further explain each point giving a clear example of what it is I am specifically looking for.

1) **The condition and operation of all of the main doors and windows.**

This point has already been touched on somewhat in the previous paragraphs and may seem quite self-explanatory but let's look at it in a little more depth. You need to check ALL the windows in the property, but in particular, the ones at the back or side of the property. You are looking for any single glazed, old aluminium or wood double glazed windows and any that have misted or failed.

I always ask the agent if they are aware of when the windows were replaced. Just like a gas boiler or a felt roof, windows have life-spans too, asking the question not only lets you plan for the inevitable future event but also and if necessary, enables you to add this cost to your overall renovation budget.

Another plus to having this information is that it may be used as leverage when it comes to the negotiation if you decide to purchase the property.

Windows and doors can be costly so it may not surprise you to learn that more often than not homeowners only replace them incrementally and often leave bathroom or cloakroom windows altogether. Front and back doors sometimes go untouched or are only ever improved if they form the visible part of the property whether that's the front or the back as in the case of overlooked properties. Be sure to note all windows are double glazed and that the operation of each is of good order.

Like mentioned earlier take note of the south-facing windows as these have a tendency to mist or fail to show condensation in between the panes. This is a real pain and can really put prospective tenants off. It is a relatively inexpensive problem to solve, but if the windows are of a certain age, it may be false economy to just simply replace the pains. If in doubt of the age ask the agent to actually find out from the vendor when the windows were replaced and if they were fitted by a FENSA registered company or installer. This is not a legal requirement but rather a guideline; however, it will give you peace of mind that they were fitted to a specific specification. It will give details of any warranty left on the installation and again offer a little more insight into the vendor's overall respect for the property over the years.

It's perhaps worth mentioning here that as of the 1st of April 2018 all rented properties needed to have an energy rating of E and above. Having good windows can dramatically improve energy performance.

2) The condition of carpets and the presence of underlay

Not having to replace carpets and underlay can potentially save you a few quid when buying a rental property.

If the carpets are in good condition, and unless they are of a patterned nature or are bright green then it is a good idea simply to get them professionally cleaned rather than going to the expense of replacing. It's a safe bet that these carpets are better quality than the ones most landlords tend to put in their rentals. If the carpets are of a certain age and you believe that replacing would be the better option here then feel the quality under your feet, has underlay been used? Again, underlay lasts a long time, and you can, in most cases avoid the extra cost of replacing it if it's still in a reasonable condition.

The use of underlay is a massively overlooked feature in the property industry. I see so many landlords spending a fortune renovating, adding extensions or converting lofts, installing new kitchens and bathrooms but then skimping right at the end of their renovation on painting and flooring. This is something I think the tenant can really pick up on, it screams 'tight landlord' over 'comfort and warmth' and will put a prospective tenant off to a degree. Ok, maybe not put them off, what I suppose I mean is that having the underlay will improve your chances of getting the best possible tenant. It may not put tenants off directly, but it almost certainly won't go unnoticed either. If they have viewed several properties in the last few days and yours is the one with the nice comfortable flooring, then you'll be remembered and for the right reasons.

If the carpets do need replacing this should be represented in your valuation and should be noted or mentioned when making your offer. Always budget a little over for the carpets when using it as a negotiation tool as the price you will pay will no doubt be lower than what the vendor would have paid but they will not realise this so let them absorb the deficit rather than you.

Again something to mention here is that I would always suggest going for a better quality, hard wearing carpet that is washable than a cheap felt backed un-washable carpet.

This approach will almost certainly save money in the long run; carpets can look old very fast in rented properties if they are not taken care of the way they should be, and trust me when I tell you that no matter how good your tenant may be they will not look after that carpet as though they would if they had paid for it themselves.

A good deep clean however, can spring a decent standard carpet back to life in no time which beats the expense of removing, disposing of, organising and then paying to replace the cheap carpet only to repeat this over again every few years.

Cheap carpets fray, shrink and wear fast so don't be fooled into thinking that you can get five-ten years out of your cheap budget carpets.

3) The walls, ceilings and their coverings

Are the walls covered with wood chip or textured backing paper, commonly known as blown vinyl? Are they covered floor to ceiling in bright red flowery wallpaper, are the children's bedrooms painted deep blue or bright pink and are the ceilings covered in aertex throughout. Does the bathroom or kitchen have wood panelling or brown patterned tiles? Are the walls plaster finished or backing papered and covered in chips or scratches or are they badly textured due to poor plastering. In essence, do they require work, or will they require work in the future and to what extent?

This work can be time-consuming, laborious and expensive. If the walls are covered with textured wallpaper its worth a little investigating if possible. Is it because it ties in with the style or age of the décor or is it because the walls are that bad underneath it was the cheapest way to cover them.

Most of the time you'll never see until you remove this, but a quick run of the hand along the wall can give an indication in some cases. Are you ready for this, have you budgeted for this, can you afford it if the entire property needs stripping and then plastering.

Do you intend on leaving this until you've accrued rent or until the initial tenancy ends, maybe you hope the tenant is going to help with this? These are all possible scenarios and should be reflected in your valuation.

4) The condition, standard and age of the kitchen and tiling. The implications of replacing and my best guess to when that would be necessary, and at what cost

What is your overall, general impression of the kitchen?

Ok, so it's a rented property at the end of the day and not your own home, so we don't expect you to fall in love with it and begin to remodel your own kitchen accordingly. But, it does have to adhere to a certain standard, after all this is going to be someone's home, and it is something that will dramatically reflect the rentability of the property. Does it have an old, or tired feel to it? Is it dark oak or white wood, is it laminated, is the laminate still intact or splitting from the edges.

Do you think it was a cheap kitchen when it was initially installed and has now well surpassed its sell-by date?

Can you see that it was a good quality kitchen in its day, but maybe it's just a little old now, but overall it's in good condition, and the carcases are solid and clean. This may aid a cheaper refurbishment by simply replacing the doors and handles but leaving the carcasses in situ.

Are the worktops suitable, in good condition and of a neutral colour or does it a deep green flex in line with the old cream and green flowery tiles. Are the tiles used just as a splash back or do they cover the entire wall making it more costly to remove and replace when necessary. If the doors are wooden and not laminated are they plain or at the very least a semi-modern design that may look ok with a modern colour applied to them.

I have had many kitchen doors painted from a light or dark oak colour to a modern sage or cream colour and by replacing the worktop, sink and handles it completely transformed the kitchen. There are kitchen companies out there now offering kitchen makeovers rather than full renovations. The reason you may opt to make the kitchen over rather than replacing it is that some replacements simply would not be cost-effective for a rental. We have some properties with huge kitchens and therefore many units so even a budget kitchen would cost 4-5k. If the carcases are in good condition inside and the implications to completely remove and replace the kitchen due to its size and intricacy would run too far into your budget then a makeover may be the best way to approach this. Again all of this will be reflected in your assessment and valuation of the property.

5) The condition, standard and age of the bathroom and tiling. The implications of replacing and my best guess to when that would be necessary, and at what cost

The same applies for the bathroom in the judging of its quality and suitability, bearing in mind however you can't paint a bath or toilet so there is not a great amount you can do to improve its appearance especially with the old cream, or coloured suites. You should be looking at the age and condition of the fixtures and the condition and feel of the tiles. A semi-modern three piece suite which includes a bath, basin and W/C with a part tiled wall along the length and width of the bath will be far cheaper to replace than an older style suite.

These often incorporate a sturdy cast iron bath, an old style low-level toilet where the waste comes to far from the wall to fit a modern close coupled cistern without the need for boxing or major plumbing work to alter the soil pipe.

Are the walls tiled floor to ceiling with a covering of 5-inch square tiles making it more time consuming to remove and subsequently more costly to replace.

Is there an old electric shower on the wall, no extractor fan and the ceiling is covered in wood panelling giving no indication of the condition beneath. You should take all this into account, and if you feel the room meets your definition of an acceptable rentable bathroom, you should still be aware of the implications to change and give your best guess as to when that may be. A bathroom can be modernised somewhat cheaper if the suite is white and in good condition rendering it suitable for re-use. Replacing fixtures or fittings like taps or wastes, renewing blinds, flooring and tiling without going to the upheaval of removing the fixed plumbing features will save both time and money.

Look for the presence of a shower, either separate from the bath or over the bath. I don't particularly like showers in rentals but unfortunately what I like doesn't seem to matter much as tenants seem to want them, especially in three- or four-bedroom properties where the probability of children and usage is high.

A shower over the bath is perfectly adequate, it doesn't have to be a separate enclosure but always look at the implications of fitting a shower if there is not one present.

Look out for ease of installation, i.e. does the back of the bath sit against a wall backing onto a landing cupboard housing a water supply. Are the walls solid or stud as a solid wall will make the job of installing a shower much more costly.

In essence, look for the closest water supply and visualise a route to your shower, being electric or mixer. Can this be done easily or does this involve removing tiles, chasing walls or coming surface mounting pipework.

Remember a mixer shower will need both a hot and cold supply whereby an electric shower will only need a cold supply, however, the latter will also need an independent cable running from the consumer unit. If this looks costly, you can always consider a bath shower mixer tap as a minimum, especially if the property incorporates a combination boiler as the hot water is fed from the mains and therefore pressure balanced to the cold supply.

6) The overall size of the bedrooms, in particular, the smallest bedroom

This is one of the most important aspects for me, most other aspects of the property can be repaired, replaced or improved but the sizes of the bedrooms are often governed by the staircase or the general layout of the upstairs.

Although I acknowledge that this can be altered somewhat, the reality is, except in the case of an extension to add value, it won't be.

You should gauge the size of the master bedroom and check its available space when there is a double bed, standard wardrobe, chest of draws and side tables installed at a minimum, if in doubt take a tape measure with you. I stipulate that the second and third bedroom both should have space for a double bed and a wardrobe unless there are built in cupboards. Obviously, the area around this will be limited, but when a single bed is installed, which will be probable, there will then be adequate space.

The fourth bedroom needs to house a single bed comfortably with space for a wardrobe only. If you have a fifth bedroom then what are you doing reading this book, have I not taught you anything, sell this immediately and invest more wisely.

Having bedrooms that are too small may not be a problem on a viewing or even when the tenant first moves in, they will often tell you that it will be fine and they will manage. However, the lack of space will quickly become apparent spurring the tenant to look for a more suitable property. A property that suited a young family in the beginning when the children were young and sharing a room soon becomes cramped when the children age and grow, and anyone who has had children will tell you "don't they grow up so fast".

The bedroom size is something you simply can't alter, if the only problem with the property lay with the age of the bathroom or kitchen, then you could easily replace these, but the size of bedrooms and in particular the smallest bedroom cannot be overstated here.

I have viewed properties that claim to have "3-bedrooms" but upon viewing it becomes apparent that it's either two medium bedrooms and a box room with hardly enough space for a single bed let alone anything else or the vendor has split the main bedroom into two bedrooms back to back and used what was the second bedroom as the master in order to try to increase the properties value.

I always assume that my 2/3 bedroom properties are going to have a minimum of two or three single occupants.

By this I mean all the bedrooms are to be used. This is a good way of approaching it as the reality may be only two bedrooms are used initially, and the third is either a study or a playroom. This heartens longevity at the property somewhat and if the worst case scenario prevails, and the family have a new arrival or great aunty Margaret moves in then the property remains suitable thereafter.

Some mitigation on that last comment, when I state that a new arrival is the worst case, I mean 'worst case' for me or us as landlords or investors and in losing a good tenant only.

I have four children, none of which are teenagers yet, so at the moment I am still quite fond of them all.

7) The age and type of central heating system installed

My best advice right at the start of this point is to do a little research, it's very easy to do and can save you thousands. As already explained agents are sometimes a little obtuse when it suits them, I think they sometimes assume that buyers are impressed with the term 'centrally heated' as they often use this in their advertising bumf.

Word of caution here though, be careful and don't let the terminology fool you.

NEWS FLASH, central heating is NOT a new method of heating a home, it started way back in the late 60's early 70's so, in essence, it's been around over 50 years. That's half a century, and I'm pretty sure this is something that we should all expect these days and not something that should be used as a pro-marketing tool.

Some boilers may have been replaced several times since the property was built, but it's often the case that the boiler was the only component replaced. The pipework and radiators may still be the original installation from way back then.

Look for old style round top or seam top radiators with 15,000 coats of paint applied.

Look for old brass type valves with grey plastic heads, these valves are without the more modern chrome coating applied. Look for old thin pipe work called microbore, this is often 10mm or 8mm in diameter. This microbore pipe can be a great indicator of the age of the initial system, and it can lead to blockages further down the line from poor circulation and therefore lower efficiency in the household.

Ideally, you want nice thick pipework supplying newer style radiators; these radiators often have grilled covers around the perimeter and fins on the back or in between the two panels called convectors.

The pipework that feeds them should ideally be 15mm which is about the thickness of the old Pentel N50 permanent marker pens or a standard stick of Blackpool rock. The pipework should lead to good modern looking chrome coloured valves that are thermostatically controlled on one side in all the main rooms. It is always a good idea to note the type of system installed in the property. If the property is four bedrooms or less, there is a good chance that when the system was replaced it was also changed or upgraded to a combination boiler type system.

This is a boiler that heats the water instantly eliminating the need for stored hot water. this is evident with the exclusion of the big square tank or tubular shaped cylinder in the airing cupboard or loft. If you are in any doubt ask the agent or vendor what system is installed and when the boiler was last replaced. If the boiler has been replaced but still uses the old storage method of water as mentioned above then find out if the external components like the storage cylinder, pump and diverter valve were replaced when the boiler was renewed. In most cases, it's simply not good enough replacing the boiler without the external components.

The reason I told you to tread carefully was that some might be forgiven, if after the agent tells you it has a modern type central heating system installed fed by a combination boiler, that you feel at ease. Again, however, combination boilers are not a new thing, I was installing combination boilers in 1999, and they were not all that new then, in fact, Worcester Bosch launched a combination boiler in 1973. They may not have been all that new in 1999, but one thing they most emphatically were was of poor quality and only designed to last about 10-15 years at best. In April 2005 a new energy efficiency law came into effect meaning that it was against regulations to fit any boiler being a combination or system boiler that was not a condensing model. Also in the same year, all boiler installations had to be registered with the building regulations department.

The property may have a 'new' type system fed by a combination boiler, but that is not to say that it is a condensing model. This means that the boiler is at best case 12-13 years old and therefore really could do with being replaced in the short term. Secondly, it may be installed onto an existing 40-year-old system which has its own obvious implications.

The best approach here is to ask the agent to provide the building regulations certificate. If this cannot be produced, then you know the boiler was either installed before 2005 or has been illegally installed thereafter. Either way, it's something you need to be aware of and can again be used as a bargaining tool if so desired. I have an engineering background specialising in gas engineering, so my course of action may be somewhat different to yours, but I would always advise that if you decide to offer on a property, you get the central heating system checked out by your own trusted professional, and not the homeowners.

In general, a gas engineers loyalty will lie with the bill payer, and it may be that his report or opinion can be vague or biased. Almost everyone knows a gas engineer these days, so there is half a chance its checked over by the brother of the guy he knows from down the club or an engineer who has served the family for years.

The best option is to note the make and model of the boiler and type that into Google you'll quickly determine its age of manufacture and be able to read the many reviews available. Just like cars, models of boilers tend to change every five years or so, this means it should be relatively easy to obtain a rough idea of its year of production. Even the so-called modern condensing models that were fitted right after the regulations changed in 2005 will all be coming up for renewal sometime soon.

Just replacing the boiler on a good system will not break the bank but again it can always be used as a bargaining tool. The vendor will already be aware of its age, so by mentioning it in your assessment of the property, you will be highlighting something he probably knew was coming anyway.

7) The age and type of consumer unit installed

Another significant cost implication here and somewhat similar to the heating system in many ways. A lot of consumer units or 'fuse boxes' as you might know them as have been updated to a modern unit with trip fuses, but the original or old wiring may have been left as in the case of the central heating pipework.

Again any alterations or upgrades need to be registered with the governing bodies and will come with a compliance certificate so get as much detail from that as possible. It can be a little harder to spot since the majority of the system is concealed under floors and in walls but look for the obvious signs like older fittings, old style sockets, switches and pull chords. If someone had the property rewired it is safe to assume that they would not put their old accessories back on.

Look for the old wire type fuse boxes; there is almost no chance that the wiring has been updated without the fuse box.

Re-wiring a property and supplying a new consumer unit can be just as if not more expensive than central heating and will in most cases certainly cause more upheaval as walls need to be chased to hide cables rather than pipe trunking which is generally accepted in central heating installations.

Look for new modern looking fuse boxes with labelled fuses; a good indication is lots of individual fuses rather than 4 or 5 along the unit. The more modern the system is and the more improvement to its internal wiring throughout the property the more need for separate fuses.

Once again and being at risk of sounding patronising, if in doubt contact your electrician and ask him to investigate or inspect the installation. This may come at a higher cost than a central heating report due to the complexity of work and time implication, but it is well worth the extra cost. You can use this report to appease your tenant of the condition of the system thereafter, and since unlike gas safety inspections it is not currently law to produce one for electrical safety your tenant will be assured that you are a trustworthy landlord to boot.

Don't be fooled simply by the presence of trip switches, however, this again is not a modern thing, this method of protection has been around for years. The new regulations state that all consumer units are made from metal rather than plastic, so if you spot one that is metal then you know, at least on the unit that you are on to a winner.

8) The size of the gardens, the areas of grassed, paved and fenced parts and the number of trees or large shrubs

These are all idyllic aspects of a property, we all love the idea of a big garden with a patio area, a front grassed lawn with a big drive, established shrubs in the garden and a 6-foot high fence around the perimeter of our property. The reality that becomes apparent once you have them, however, is the daunting relentless task of maintenance. A large garden may be a huge pull when trying to find a tenant with a family. A front garden looks lovely when freshly cut and will impress when showing a prospective tenant around. A nice weed free patio area may look inviting with some garden furniture laid out, but go back and look a few months later when the patio has sprouted its own version of an allotment and the front garden since it's never used is resembling something similar to a wild meadow.

A year on, the back garden will in most cases look more like the rough on an under-maintained golf course rather than the bowling green it was when you bought the property.

Fences that are in poor condition can be a real nuisance on windy days, the type of which we have many of here in the UK, they can come with a pretty hefty cost to replace when the time comes also.

On semi-detached and or terraced properties it's worth finding out whose boundary and therefore responsibility the fences are part of, but even then, that should not necessarily appease you there is no guarantee that they will be replaced as and when you would ideally like them to be.

I don't want to sound too pessimistic about these things, but Instead of looking for the idyllic scenarios I look for the practicalities of the property. I look for good sized but low maintenance gardens with either a pebbled or paved area that are both flat and even and ideally with cemented joints which help to keep the weed situation down.

My advice is to try to minimise the grassed areas as much as possible, especially at the front of the property. I know from my own experience that these get left or overlooked. I have a front garden at my own property, and it is an absolute chore to cut. I generally cut it every other time when cutting the back garden, and I am a workaholic, next doors front grass gets cut every other year!

Look for gardens that have either very few or very low maintenance shrubs or flowers or even consider removing them entirely if this property is the one.

You'll find that trees get out of control rather quickly and instead of being the pleasure they were intended when planted they will become the pain I suggest above. I Look for gardens that have clearly been maintained by the property's owner. You'll eventually, if you intend on becoming a professional or keen investor, get to a level where you walk into a garden and a very pleasing smile will grace your face when you see a good solid, well looked after painted fence that encloses a pebbled garden with a small grassed area to the rear and a clean patio housing small shrubs and plants all contained in large clay pots.

The front is very similar, the smaller the front garden, the better and I like no grass at all as it becomes a pain for 95% of the tenants out there. This is especially the case in some terraced properties where the mower has to be carried through the property. Therefore the resulting factor here is that it gets kicked to the back of the priority list and in most cases left to weed and seed rather than weed and feed.

I preferably like my front areas to be fenced, but this must be of solid construction using good thick treated wood, not something that is going to be blown over in light winds. You'd be surprised how many calls we get the day after a light storm, it's got to the point where my wife gets the "wonder how many calls you'll get tomorrow" comment in before I do.

In summary look for low maintenance, practical areas over idyllic gardens that will require ongoing maintenance. Our management company has recently taken control of a property that has a huge back garden; The entire perimeter is boarded by conifer, hawthorn and other such trees or bushes. It has a huge Oaktree at the bottom and is surrounded by another three gardens with similar plantings all hanging over and filling in the gaps like a well-built fortress wall. This sounds lovely in an idyllic sense, it's extremely spacious and very private. However, this has just cost the owner a little over £750 to trim and dispose of and will cost somewhere in that region year on year to maintain. The rent on this property is £550 now that's the equivalent of the property being empty for almost six weeks every year. This is a bad enough hit when the property is tenanted but factor in the typical 10% void and a nominal maintenance fee, it becomes somewhat of an issue going forward! Not the best purchase in the world huh? It's a shame my book wasn't available when it was sourced.

9) The drive or parking area

Much of what I mentioned above is relevant here regarding practicality and low maintenance. You should look for well-laid drives, ones that won't need replacing anytime soon, ones that are sunk or uneven or even crumbling can be costly to repair or replace.

This can be one of the most significant but unnecessary costs you can face as a landlord. At least with a new kitchen, boiler or bathroom you get something that is really improving the property and its appeal, something that will be noticeable and will aid you in your efforts in obtaining the perfect tenant, the condition of the drive is as consigned to oblivion as the front garden will be in most cases.

When it comes to the outside area of any of my rental properties, I look at them as unnecessary money pits, I loathe spending money on having trees removed, or conifers cut backed, patios re-laid, grouted or cleaned and anything similar to that effect.

Parking can be an important factor to many however, so it is a great bonus if you have a drive at the property. It is perhaps the best feature of outside space in my opinion, and although it does for me, trump any garden you'll often find that properties with drives also have decent sized gardens to boot, here with the pro also lies, the con, or potential con.

The garden can be as big as a football pitch as long as its low maintenance. It is worth thinking of the future tenant living at the property and how the parking of their car will impact their lives. For instance, if I had to park my car in a parking bay, walk down the road a little and onto a path then continue past six terraced properties to view a property, I may not give it much thought. It's only a short 30-second walk, a beautiful sunny day and I'm away with the fairies thinking of the potential cash flow of the property and how that will positively affect my life so I may not even notice.

If I am a tenant, however, and I have to make that walk twice daily at a minimum, seven days a week, 365 days a year, my views may change. I imagine pulling into the bay mid-winter when its minus two degrees, raining heavily, blowing a gale and I have to do this walk, not empty handed you understand. I have my newborn baby with me as well as the weekly shop. This may require three or four trips to empty, all while leaving my newborn baby in the living room.

Its safe to say that this short 30-second walk will soon become a tedious chore, and fast.

Also, don't be fooled when you see that parking is available roadside directly outside the property. If the property is on a long row of terraced properties and everyone along that row has a car, some even have two, parking near the property may become a daily potluck exercise, this again might impact my love of the property somewhat.

This is one of the reasons I do my plastic gangland drive-bys at various times of the day; it helps me to gauge the parking on the street or road. I have opted not to buy properties previously that would have otherwise been suitable if not for the parking. I remember quite vividly about 6 or 7 years ago when I was on the way to show one of my existing tenants around a property and her comments that changed my thinking.

I was considering purchasing this property and wanted to move her in. The property was within a cul-de-sac type area of terraced properties, and I remember pulling up to the property that I was going to offer on the very next day and not being able to find anywhere to park my car. The tenant had to get out and peer through the windows of the property alone, this was mid-afternoon when the street really should be at its emptiest. Her comment upon getting back into the car was, "is it always this busy" and there it was, the epiphany. In that one comment, I withdrew my interest from the property, and I have taken note ever since.

The more bedrooms the property has, the more this will impact my judgement, for instance, the chances of one of the tenants owning a car in a three-bedroom household over a two-bedroom household is naturally higher. There is more chance that I will attract a family in a three-bedroom property, maybe a working family with two cars, conversely, there is a good chance that in a two-bedroom property I will attract a single unemployed parent without a car, so this should all be relative to your thinking and careful planning.

10) The roof, fascias and guttering

A lot of this has already been explained earlier on in the section, it's an area that can be visible when you either drive or walk by, or you can check as you're waiting for the agent to turn up at the viewing. As a recap, look for a good clean roof without a massive build-up of moss or other such matter or any cracked or slipped tiles, each row of tiles should be uniform to the roofline. Look for a good solid straight roof line with no dips along the ridge.

The fascia's should ideally be upvc and be solid looking. The same applies to the guttering, it should run uniform to the roofline again without dips but pay close attention to the horizontal jointing, and the vertical downcomers. Any signs of moss build-up on the joints and or staining of the adjacent bricks needs to be investigated when viewing internally.

Damp can cause all sorts of problems and needs addressing as soon as it's discovered. Look for any signs of the walls being washed internally near joints, this may be represented by a cleaner area of the wall, or the paint may have run with the applied water. Either way, it is a good indication that the joint has been left leaking for some time and the water has penetrated through the wall. Although this is a relatively easy repair and the wall will dry out over time, it is again a good indication of the way the vendor has looked after the property over the years.

11) Other boards, either to-let or for sale
Now that you're becoming engrossed in property and either buying or considering buying, you'll be aware of things you were not aware of prior to this. One of these will be the abundance of For Sale and To-Let boards around.

This is a good thing and like I mentioned at the start of the book you will notice properties or areas that you never considered before all from these boards; you'll get a subconscious understanding of rental areas, areas in demand and areas that are overpopulated with landlord's vacant properties.

This brings me precisely to the point, point 12 on my list. If I see an area with a lot of to-let and for sale boards erected, I see a connecting string of alarm bells attached.

Either the area is overpopulated with landlords creating an overload of supply and subsequently a reduced rental price or an abundance of empty properties or, worse it's a poor area with a high turnover of tenants, and although the demand is there, the quality tenants are not.

This is why I generally stay away from areas that have a high mix of these boards.

Either one or the other, like a few To-Let or a few For Sale boards independently of each other, may not be so bad, it can easily be and should be investigated further. There may be a genuine reason for the boards individually, but if I see a mixture of both, then I dismiss without investigation these days.

Many years' of experience being a private landlord, professional investor and running the lettings agency has given me this cautious approach. I've mentioned before, and I feel its right to mention, here again, properties come along all the time, by dismissing these overpopulated streets you will be saving yourself from the potential heartache of an empty asset.

Within a few weeks, you'll have moved on to another more suitable and profitable street or area, completely forgetting about the last one.

12) Anything else major, noticeable or unusual that jumps out at me

I know my local area very well, and I know the common problems that some of the properties in certain areas have. For instance, there are areas of my town that require mandatory floor tests as the floors in some areas contain shale or other such substances that lenders don't particularly like. I know that some of the pitched roofs are retrofitted or additions over the old flat concrete roofs.

I know that the next town over to me has significant problems with damp or ventilation issues and even slight subsidence in some areas. You may not know your area initially in the way I do, I had the benefit of coming from a trade background, which gave me this underpinning knowledge before I started investing. I had worked for many years in these properties and talked with many of the landlords about the problems they faced.

Anything major, noticeable or unusual for you should include signs of damp which is easily recognised by flaking paint, wet or moulding paper, signs of water marks on the wall or the darkening of the walls in the corners of the rooms, usually at a low level.

Look for cracks in walls, don't worry too much about cracks in plasterboard along joint lines or similarly on the ceiling but instead cracks that are not uniform and are predominantly on solid walls.

In particular, ones that are large enough to poke a screwdriver in comfortably, this can be a sign of subsidence or poor workmanship. Like always, if in doubt, get these checked out by your trusted professional or simply walk away from the property.

Broken record I know but another property will come along before you know it.

Look for uneven floors, floors upstairs that slope away from one side to the other, concrete floors that blister up in certain areas or are loose underfoot.

Always look in the neighbour's gardens and note the activity, a garden filled with rubbish or other unwanted material scattered around an overgrown jungle or an old couch under the window at the front of the property can quickly highlight that the neighbours of the property are not exactly ones that most would choose.

Look for all the signs that the neighbours are respectful of their property and surroundings and generally you'll be ok with them.

Take note of unusually small rooms, I have touched on bedroom sizes above, and I think that is a very important factor. I tend not to notice the downstairs as much; this is because I generally buy three-bedroom properties, so you'll find that these often have decent living areas downstairs.

I recognise that not all of you will buy three-bedroom properties as with my strategy, so this next point is perhaps worth mentioning.

You'd be surprised how much people spend on flat screen TV's and how ridiculously big they are, couple that with a large corner couch and your smaller than average living room will struggle to house these 'must have' items.

Regardless of the potential in the kitchen this quickly becomes a major issue when sourcing a tenant.

Note however, I have found that the Eastern European tenants don't mind the living rooms being small so much, furthermore, they actually prefer the kitchen to be larger in comparison or even as a sacrifice to the smaller living space. This is because their culture revolves a lot more around food and the social aspects of food rather than TV and the anti-social aspect of that.

Look for the location of sockets or more accurately look for an inherent lack of them in some rooms. This can prove a problem when your tenant moves in only to find that their bedroom houses only one double socket.

This is not nearly enough for their 70" bedroom TV, bedside lamp, phone charger, laptop charger, I-pad charger, hair straightness, hair dryer, hair curlers, iPod docking station, re-chargeable electric toothbrush, electric shaver and any other devices they may want to overload your circuits with.

You should note storage areas or rather the inherent lack of them; storage areas can be a huge bonus in a property especially when the tenant is in and settled.

A lack of storage, however, can cause havoc at the exact opposite end of the spectrum, especially when trying to store hoovers, ironing boards etc.

I have been in countless properties that due to reconfigurations or extensions have no storage space whatsoever. Who wants to see their hover on a daily basis let alone step over it, not least the tenants who have little or no intention on using it.

Lastly, if it's obvious that a property has had major renovation work or extensions, check to see that it all complies with building regulations and that the owner has accountable invoices and of course permission to build. I check warranties and anything like that, I pay close attention to the structure and walls within the extension. Generally though, at the rented level this probably won't apply most of the time.

The above points should give you a good benchmark in starting to help you look for a properties suitability.

Not only to your own particular strategy but in relation to your budget, it goes without saying that some form of compromise will have to be reached. If your strategy involves renovating a property in poor condition for either re-sale or re-mortgage purposes, then some can be bypassed entirely, however even in this case the more of the list that can be checked off and forgotten about the cheaper the renovation will be. If you buy a property in need of a full cosmetic refurbishment, then realise that the heating and electrics all need replacing as well, this can seriously affect your budget and subsequent profit or release of equity.

There are other things to consider that may be relevant to your strategy or chosen area, but I believe most major points have been covered and will help guide you very well in the beginning.

Part 2 - Purchasing property
Chapter 3, Offering and negotiating

There are some books or strategies circulating that will tell you to view as many properties as possible, all at once.

Some even suggest using the laws of probability and making silly offers on them all until one gets accepted at a price that would make it a criminal offence not to purchase it.

This can and most likely will, due to circumstantial reasons actually happen if you take this approach.

If you're only intending on buying one or two properties, it's not a bad idea really, so long as they all fit your chosen strategy and are in good rentable areas.

However, if you're planning on buying several properties or intend on becoming a full-time or professional investor, then my consensus here is that this approach would grow old very fast for the agent and the subsequent relationship you are aiming to build will become near impossible as a result.

Some of the same books or strategies, mine included will tell you that you should never pull out of a deal but offering on ten properties when you only have the funds to buy two could be detrimental for obvious reasons and are in fact contradictory.

There is nothing more damaging to a relationship than taking money from another's pocket. By making the agent think that he has secured a sale, he will have subconsciously banked the sale fee.

To then let him down comes with many obvious pitfalls, the impression this will make on the agent will be one of either distrust or a lack of integrity, either way, it's a long road back.

The fundamental advice here is to only offer on a property if you intend to honour the purchase and only when you have the funds available, or you are certain that they will be available or at the very least, in place for completion.

I would suggest you adopt this respectful approach even if your current strategy is only to purchase one or two properties.

Believe it or not, I never really intended to buy more than a couple of properties initially.

Back then I was not concerned with cash flow, but instead building a retirement plan, I certainly had no intention writing a book as a professional property investor.

The point here is that if you do decide to continue to purchase property, even some years later, it is a whole lot easier if the relationship with the agent hasn't been tarnished due to a sporadic or ill-advised strategy.

I don't intend to go into too much depth in this chapter since there are so many different ways to approach and offer on a property based on many individual and variable factors.

This is especially if you intend on it being a drawn-out negotiation or an acquisition of a hugely down valued purchase.

But also and essentially I don't really think this is where the industry is heading or should really be played anymore. I'm just not an advocate of squeezing every penny from the vendor or searching scrupulously for that property that you can try to down value somewhat. I do like value for money of course, and I certainly think you should get a good deal taking into account the possible future expenditure of the property and using that well to your advantage, especially if your strategy relies on releasing equity. However, if the property is in the cheaper bracket and you intend on squeezing it further through some sort of Del-boy tactic, I believe the property, and the subsequent tenant will be a representation of this.

It is my current opinion, looking at a somewhat flooded market, that it would be to your advantage to spend an extra few grand on a great property rather than to squeeze a few extra grand on an average property. It will pay dividends in the future, and if the property is that good, the vendor and agent will know it, rendering even the best case Derran Brown tactics useless.

My opinion here is only that; It is an observational comment based on my assessment of the past few years of the industry.

It is something I currently feel strongly about, especially with the investor who has a good amount of initial capital.

This is something I go into in depth with on our training courses using the demonstration of the fundamental mathematics of the purchase as my basis for persuasion.

All the above duly noted I do however appreciate that there will be many of you out there who need to purchase at the best possible price to implement your strategy, so I will, of course not shirk my responsibilities and offer advice or opinion even if it is a little briefer than other topics.

Your offer, just as it was with contacting the agent has to be mindful of approach; you don't want to upset anyone, look too eager, miss a deal or worse, buy an overpriced property. There are means and ways in which you can do this.

As your experience and relationships grow you can be a little more truthful with the agents, after all, they'll soon understand that you're not a time waster and that your intentions are real. Your actions will demonstrate that you're a serious buyer, and when you say you'll buy a property, you do, they'll know that your timescales are appropriately matched and that the funds are in place. They'll know that you always make smooth and if needed swift purchases.

When this time arrives, the precedence will have switched, you'll have earned the right to be a bit brass or to swiftly dismiss a property within a couple of minutes without offending the agent or even offering any justification; they'll simply know that this property does not meet your criteria.

But until that time arrives, you'll have to play the tactical card somewhat.

Although I tend to do this now, you should never offer on a property during the viewing stage if you are trying to negotiate hard.
In the early days, you need to tread lightly when offering on a property. Offering during a viewing is a privilege you earn with experience and a correctly worked strategy, not something I can really teach in a book.

Offering on a property can be very straightforward if you're not trying to bend anyone, or it can be a minefield if you are.
Negotiating is not only a tactical war but a test of your understanding of psychology. You'll need to have some steel, some patience and a whole lot of resolve. Again, I will let you know what I used to do in the earlier days and sometimes still do today where necessary; this will enable you to highlight the things that you like and conversely don't like then implement these how you see them fitting into your strategy.

How you offer on a property may be governed entirely or somewhat by your strategy, but in general, it will mainly be governed by the three main factors below, these factors may be exclusive or can be interlinked or merged somewhat but will reflect in accordance to the way you act or set out your offer.

The three main factors are:
1) Is the property new to the market?
2) Has the property been on the market for a long time?
3) How much do you want the property and what are you prepared to pay for it?

1) Is the property new to the market?

When a property comes onto the market there are several things I do, what I unquestionably don't do is offer on it straight away. I wouldn't even view it straight away.

There are perhaps a few exceptions to this rule that I will explain at the end of this point, but I always wait for the dust to settle so to speak and there are good reasons for doing this.

If a property is new to the market, it will generally be overpriced or vastly under-priced to attract substantial interest for example when a property is to be sold via auction.

It will generally, even when overpriced attract some interest immediately, this interest gives both the vendor and the agent some false hope, I don't want to be part of this false hope. If I view this property, like it and offer on it, there is a very good chance due to this false hope that the offer will be rejected initially thus wasting my time or prolonging the timeframe to when the property is reduced to a more realistic price.

I would rather bide my time for others to view and either give the overpriced asking price, not offer since it was in fact overpriced or offer ridiculous amounts in the hope of getting a bargain, either way, it's a win-win situation for me, even if it sells. It means I haven't wasted any time viewing an overpriced property that I was never going to be able to secure anyway.

Once the initial interest dies off the vendor and his agent will steadily come into the wonderful world of reality. It is at this perfect point, having watched the progression on Rightmove closely, but never before the listing has been reduced as this is a clear indicator that the false hope has lapsed that I can come along and offer something that is a little more realistic to my valuation of the property, after viewing of course. This is not a strategy that needs to be employed on every property of course, just be mindful of what the correct asking price should be and if it is overpriced as in my example then be patient and wait for the listing to change

Ok, so the exception to this rule is that if the agent has put me on to the Property as it's not currently on the market or that I really like the property and I want to be first through the door as I would be willing to pay close to the asking price, even the inflated asking price for whatever reason.

This does happen more and more these days. Being an investor does have its drawbacks when viewing someone's home as often people can attach sentimental value to their home and don't want a greedy investor turning their property into a stereotypical doss- house for layabouts. However, in lots of cases it can have considerable benefits, and when a property is in high demand, this is when these benefits, along with the well-established personal relationship you have with your agent really prevail.

It provides the vendor with the comfort and confidence that the sale will materialise. You're not in a chain, and you're an experienced buyer who has immediate funds. The agent will let the vendor know that you can complete quickly and smoothly giving you the best chances of securing the property that has just come on the market, the one that everybody wants.

I've been fortunate enough on a few occasions to buy property when I wasn't the highest bidder, but the seller had been let down previously, and since the agent had assured him that the sale would categorically proceed, I secured the purchase, and at the correct price.

2) Has the property been on the market for a long time?

The game here is not timing anymore since the vendor, and quite possibly the agent has lost any sign of false hope but rather how desperate you think the vendor now is. When I offer on a property, I generally and purposely wait for the agent to call me for my feedback. Usually, they do this the day after the viewing, but in this scenario, I don't mind viewing the property and offering soon after *(only under exceptional circumstances would you ever call the agent to offer on a property).*

The game now is in fact price, and your offer should reflect the properties foundations on Rightmove.

Given the fact that the property has been on the market for a good while, and by a good while and judging by my local area I generally mean longer than two or three months. I am assuming that you want to view since all your research either points to some potential that others have failed to see or that you just rather like the area and feel it makes for a good investment. Either way, you have used careful due diligence and have decided that you'd rather like to purchase the property.

There is a good chance that the property has some major pitfalls, enough to put people off for such a prolonged timeframe, so before you view you need to be aware of these and note everything that you feel is either a significant drawback or carries a significant cost implication. You also need to note all the pros of the property and highlight the main things that are drawing you to its purchase. After the viewing, you need to work out your maximum purchase price and then format the list I just mentioned. This requires formatting in a way that demonstrates the main cost implications at the top in one column and the main draws at the top in the other column. When the agent approaches you for your feedback and asks if you intend to offer it's time to recite your list.

The trick here is to note two things you like about the property, this could be the area or the low maintenance garden then mention two or three of the more significant drawbacks. The drawbacks should be the ones that carry the most significant costs. Then either reaffirm the first two pro's or throw in another positive, maybe that you know it will rent well since your research shows the demand is strong.

The reason you do this, and I am sure you will be aware of what the term is for this metaphorical sandwich is so that your assessment looks like a well-balanced overview of the property rather than a big list of negatives aimed at drawing the price down. It also shows a well thought out process that demonstrates your ability to assess a properties saleability which will give you a better chance of securing purchases in the future.

This list is designed to take the agent on a little psychological journey; it makes them feel you like the property, initially giving them hope. It then brings them back down to earth with the reality they already know which is the extent or implications of the project, then taking them back up a notch with the affirmation that on the whole you rather like the property despite the pitfalls, but you do intend to factor these into your offer.

You can then offer in two ways; the first is the, I don't really want the property but would take it on for the right price method.

In this method, you tell the vendor that although you quite liked the property, on the whole, you didn't really want to take on the renovations needed or the initial financial costs due to the renovations required are a little too high.

Their response will almost certainly be to ask you what you would be prepared to pay. It is at this point you reply with your X valuation of the property.

This should be a fraction under the maximum you are prepared to pay so that there is no negotiating. This demonstrates that you're not angling for any reduction. If the agent comes back with a counteroffer from the vendor, I always maintain resolve and never deviate from my stance.

It is a common perception that negotiations start low to high respectively and then meet somewhere in the middle, however standing firm shows you're serious. Often the agent will relay your stance once again to the vendor and return with the call of acceptance the second time around.

The reason I mention that it is to be a fraction under the asking price and I do mean a fraction, perhaps a few hundred pounds, is that often to win these negotiations there is perhaps some give needed, simply so that the other side feels they have won some little battle.

The second method is the 'I only have certain funds available' method; this is to tell the agent that although you like the property the renovations required means that your budget and funds determine your offer of X, this avoids upsetting anyone with a low offer as you have provided sufficient caveats to mitigate this.

This offer should either be a few thousand or a certain percentage under your maximum purchase price, in the case of the vendor returning with a counter you can always inform them that you may be able to loan or find extra funds in order to proceed after you've stood firm of course.

Either method has a good chance of being successful since the prolonged period on the market means that the agent's priority lies in selling the property at your offered amount rather than the vendors preferred amount. The result is that the agent will do what they can to work for you in a way that helps to convince the vendor that the sale should proceed.

3) How much do I want the property

This is a tricky one, it does get easier in time with the more properties you view and the more you purchase.

Initially, you will be a little rushed, maybe scared of losing out on the 'perfect property' and despite my relentless advice on patience, you may go all guns blazing to secure the purchase.

There is nothing overly wrong with that providing your research is thorough, and it's a good solid property in a rentable location.

However as time goes on, particularly in relation to the volume of viewings you are attending you will realise or begin to realise that there are so many other properties on the market just like this one, and if that's not the case at present, there will be soon enough, trust me on that one.

There are various routes you can take when a property really takes your fancy, but they will all be determined by your available funds, overall strategy and need or desire to progress at that moment in time.

A prime example of this being; let's assume you have readily available funds for a couple of purchases and you are really only intending on buying a couple of solid properties for a small retirement pot.

You really, really like this property, let's say the property is in a desirable area, it's a good low maintenance plot and has been refurbished or improved to a good standard over the years.

All the outside areas are in good order, and it's only been on the market a short while. Indeed if this is the case, it makes no sense to play any mind games, phycological trickery or haggle with the vendor to any real extent. In this instance I would suggest offering what you see fit, there is no point in me trying to educate you on the negotiating tactic as it is somewhat Inconsequential to your desired outcome here. Just bear in mind that the agent will always place the property for sale slightly higher than what the vendor is willing to accept.

Usually, they would add say between 5-10% as a benchmark, however the lower the property value, the more this figure changes but for the purpose of average rentals, it is safe to assume this as a circa.

The above approach is actually something I advocate for those with readily available funds or perhaps adopting a steadier strategy; it forms the general basis of my current strategy since I am in no immediate rush or in fact have any more targets, I feel I need to hit, having achieved them some years ago.

If however you really like the property but you feel it is a little overpriced, or your budget does not stretch quite far enough. Maybe you do intend to renovate and are aware that every thousand pound in the buying process is a thousand pound lost on the remortgage or resale of the property. There are a few tricks or techniques you can try here. The first thing you need to do, even before you view is to determine how much you want or more specifically can pay for the property; this is a simple exercise determined again by your strategy and also using the methods we talked about in the last chapter. The first thing you need to do is to inform the agent of your position, make them aware that you really like the property, you're in a strong chain free position to proceed, but unfortunately, your budget does not stretch to the full asking price. This is either because your deposit is not large enough or you feel there are X amount of costs involved throughout your specific refurbishment plan that has not been accounted for in their valuation.

If this is the case just be completely honest, upfront, transparent, and only tell a little white lie. Using a similar approach to the one above, give the vendor some of the positives about the property. Tell them you like the area, the kitchen or the layout then give him a couple of the negatives like "but the bathroom will need replacing along with the carpets to make the property rentable" then finish affirming that you really do want the property, obviously at a price that matches your income.

You then bring out the little white lie and offer a certain percentage below what your circumstances deem your maximum offer to be, affirming your love of the property but indicating that this is your absolute maximum offer due to your current circumstances. An example would be a £105,000 property is on the market in need of some minor cosmetic work, not too dissimilar to what was mentioned above. New carpets, bathroom and some minor cosmetics runs at about £4,000, let's assume you have done your research and you know the price is fitting for the area and the property but the maximum you could pay, bearing in mind the fees associated and the renovation costs, would be £98,000 you would then go in with an offer of £95,000 and let the agent do his job and work the deal for you, if you've been convincing in your love for the property but highlighted the pitfalls he will relay this information to the vendor in full, he will know that you really want the property and believe me when I tell you he will want the sale, he will be able to smell it and he will use all of his sales and persuasive techniques on the vendor to push it through. He will make it very clear that you have offered the maximum amount you can, and this will help sway the vendor.

So, what if the vendor refuses and the agent comes back with a rejection? Well, he will at this point because he has tried his very hardest and does not now after being able to taste the sale want it to fall through give you some indication of the vendors lowest price, maybe he comes back and tells you that the vendor is not in a position to take anything less than £102,000 due to his onward chain or personal finances, ok so you thank the agent for his time and because it is out of your reach you do actually walk away and continue your search. But if the agent comes back and indicates that the vendor is able to sell closer to £98,500 because of his current position or financial status, then we can continue our pursuit. At £98,500 the property is affordable, but you have told the agent that your maximum affordable offer was £95,000. You again reaffirm the love of the property but tell them that it is such a shame to miss out for a few grand, thank them for their time and make them aware that the offer is on the table indefinitely while you still have the funds available. This will provoke action, and a few things can happen, the agent will return the feedback to the vendor, and the vendor will now realise that you were serious with your maximum bid and that he, although lower than he wanted has lost a potential sale. Maybe the vendor needs the sale as his mortgage term is up, perhaps he will lose his place in the chain, perhaps he is downsizing, and there is a lot of profit in the sale, whatever the reason he will start to question if the sale is worth a few grand. The next vital thing to do is to be patient. The agent will either come back to you in a day or so and accept your offer or maybe come in with an offer that is close to yours but still leaves the vendor happy. Or nothing will happen, in this case, a few days have passed, and you know the vendor is not going to change his mind; you then call the office and ask about the progress.

Always, if possible, talk with the agent that showed you around the property, he already knows your feelings and position on the property; it will just make things easier. You can then do one of two things, you can meet the offer or continue playing hardball and inform him that you've been able to secure a loan from a family member so you can up your bid to £96,500 in most cases the bid will succeed as the vendor is not going to want to lose the sale twice especially for a couple of grand, but really in essence do you? if this bid gets turned down then come back in with your third and final bid, this one is a random number like £97,653; the buyer will now know this is make or break, nine times out of ten you'll secure the deal. I have to admit this final random number strategy is one that has only recently been brought to my attention by another professional investor I have been working with, I haven't actually used it myself but would have many times over the years had I known about it, it is simple and effective, and carries a definite meaning.

If you really like the property and all your research confirms your suspicions that it's a great buy my advice is to offer somewhere near its marketed value, maybe less 6% or 7% providing the comparables stack up somewhere in accordance with your offer

At the start of point 3, I mentioned that it is was a funny one and that it gets easier, and it really does. It's a funny one because really for things to progress, there is not a lot to be said in getting a property for below market value or BMV. I mean what is BMV it is only a reflection of the market at the current time. Markets can sway and often do on a yearly basis, you may pay £100,000 for a £105,000 property but in 18-months time the property may be worth £98,000 but again what does that really matter? Unless you intend to sell, i.e. you bought the property as a flip or remortgage after renovation since this is your strategy then really the price you pay is relatively insurmountable in the scheme of things or looking at the broader or longer-term picture. These days I can't really be bothered to haggle too much if I don't intend on renovating to refinance in the near future. If the property is on for £90,000, I know the agent has told the vendor that he will advertise it at £90,000 with a view to taking offers around £87,000 so I offer £85,000 and, in most cases, end up buying. What I will say to finish is, if you're intending on being a professional or semi-professional investor never buy with your heart, always your mind and use due diligence. If you're buying a property for your retirement pot then fine, buy the property you love, buy it, love it and maintain it in a pleasurable manner keeping your tenant happy in the process. If you look after the property and are selective with your screening of tenants, then you should have a great little retirement pot.

Part 2 - Purchasing property

Chapter 4, The financials

Over the course of the book, I have demonstrated some rough examples of the purchasing costs in order to highlight certain points I was trying to make. They omitted relevant areas or fees relating to the purchase to aid with continuation or simplicity and so not to deter from my overall point. I also didn't want to bombard you with an overload of information, particularly overwhelming information so early on in the book.

I did promise however that I would highlight the full costs involved in buying a property later on in the book, and now that we are well into the abyss of detail that time has come.

This chapter will give you a full insight and make clear the costs associated with purchasing a property; I intend to walk you through an entire purchase with regards to the financials, starting with your broker and finishing with the final payment to your solicitor.

Before I do that, I want to discuss the options briefly that you have available to purchase property, that being through the vessel in which to purchase, mainly through a personal type portfolio or through a limited company which seems to be trending now.

I say briefly as this really is something you should approach your accountant about, they are in a far better position than me to advise you on what to do. I just want to offer a quick and definite unaccountable overview of the two main options which may, or may not, help shed some light on the saga.

The two main options are:

1) to purchase the property personally
2) to purchase through a limited company

Buying property through a personal avenue is what many investors, myself included used to do but now since the government has put a gradual block on the way higher rate taxpayers are able to offset interest payments from mortgages over the next few years it is becoming more the case that investors are purchasing property through their limited companies.

In brief, you would set up a Special Purpose Vehicle (SPV) and loan your funds to the company by means of a director's loan. These loaned funds are used to purchase property through the company.
The two main benefits of this approach are that firstly you are still eligible to offset the interest payments paid to the mortgage companies against your yearly tax bill.
Secondly, you are not charged at the higher rate tax band on the profits accrued.

There are drawbacks, however, there is no capital gains allowance within a limited company, and if you're not the only shareholder in the company, you don't fully own the property either.

Mortgages can be slightly harder to obtain and are generally at a marginally higher rate than that of personal mortgages, but as more and more investors are choosing this avenue, it is becoming easier since more mortgage companies are lining up to take your money.

The governments change in regulations stated that beginning from April 2017 landlords will no longer be able to deduct their mortgage interest costs against their taxable profits.

Now if you're a higher rate taxpayer, this is going to affect you drastically as previously this offset entitled you 40% tax relief , but the new law changes mean that you lose this right altogether. Although You are no longer allowed to offset this interest against your pre-tax profits in the basic rate band either, there is a caveat.

The government have introduced something called a tax reducer of 20% off mortgage interest incurred to both tax bands which means, since basic rate taxpayers are only able to offset at 20% anyway, the net result will mean there is no change at all for them.

This is unless the removal of the interest payment deduction pushes your profit into the higher rate band.

If your mortgage is on an interest-only basis, this could be hundreds or thousands of pounds each year if you're a higher rate taxpayer, and If you've got multiple properties, then you can see the implications could be far higher here.

It means that some landlords are paying a tax bill that is higher than the actual profit accrued from their investments. The government are not bringing this in immediately but rather inclemently over a four-year period. This means you lose 25% of your allowance per year. It's not actually that simple as there are other calculations involved here, but this is why I advise going to see your accountant if you think you may be affected by this. Remember that this will only affect higher rate taxpayers. If you're currently a basic rate taxpayer, then this won't affect you at all, unless the gross figure of your investment income pushes you through the threshold. These calculations can get tricky and are often difficult to explain without the aid of a pen and paper so speak with your accountant as they will advise accordingly.

It may be helpful to some of you before I get to the bones of this chapter to tell you about my personal situation as I feel it may be relevant to a portion of the readers.

I was already running a limited company when I started buying property; this meant that I took dividend payments from my business instead of a wage, I used my tax-free allowance and paid myself the minimum amount so that my national insurance contributions were met which is an insignificant sum, I think it currently stands at £11,500. This meant that all the profit earned from my investment property initially kept me in the lower rate tax bracket, I would take my dividend from the business to take me up to the threshold after assessing my income from property.

As this could be done for my wife also, it meant that even by today's standards I could own quite a few properties before entering the higher rate tax bracket.

If I were to start buying property all over again from now, I would be able to max out my property portfolios gross profit to take me and my wife right up to the basic rate tax threshold which currently stands at £45,000 before I needed to buy property through SPV. In essence, since my wife works for our company and only draws the same minimum payment as I do, we could own property that brought in somewhere in the region of £67,000.

Based on £500/month rent that would be the equivalent of 11 properties. It is my understanding or my way of thinking that it is far better to own the properties personally than in a limited company, remember there is no limited liability on purchasing property through a limited company, you yourself will be a guarantor for the mortgage. The added benefit of owning your property personally is if the markets were to rise and we wanted to sell a few properties we are able to use our personal tax-free capital gains allowance which currently stands at £11,300 each before we pay any tax on this profit. The other encouraging factor here is that we now have a comfortable passive income from our personal portfolio and since we have built a somewhat successful company by offering a service that well surpasses our customers' expectations and relative 'paid for' service we are able to leave the accrued profits within the company.

This retained profit, in turn, builds and compounds yearly creating a deeper foundation for growth as a result and also provides surplus capital to purchase property through this vessel as another avenue for profit.

Ok back to the point.

To present an accurate representation of a purchase and its associated fees I will run you through the last purchase I made on a three-bedroom property only a few weeks ago.

I purchased the property for £68,000 via the local estate agent that I believe I have the best relationship with. I felt that the property only needed somewhere in the region of £2,500 spending on it, so it was added to my 'rentable' tab on my spreadsheet. The property was on the market for £78,000, but I knew it was slightly overpriced and it was a deceased estate, so I offered £68,000, and the vendor took it within 20 minutes of me viewing the property now this may be down to timing, my assessment of the property or my established relationship with the agent. Perhaps a mix of all three, but regardless of the reason, the methods I apply on a daily basis all do contribute to these kinds of purchases.

My first port of call was to see my broker to arrange a mortgage. Brokers sometimes offer their services to the purchaser for free as they claim their arrangement fee from the mortgage companies, but I pay my broker, and I pay her well. She does a very good job, and I value her service, The free brokers get paid by the lender by means of commission, so I tend to question loyalties here, who do you think they want to please you or the bill payer?
I know my broker works for me, as, although she receives a commission from the lender, she earns her money primarily through her clients. She is 'whole of the market' which means she has access to all the mortgage products available and is not tied to any group of lenders. Her fee is £250, £150 upon application and £100 after the mortgage has been offered.

I would question any business who offers a principally free service to its customers; I would always be wary of their hidden agenda.
I classed myself as the best gas engineer around when I ran my gas services business, so I charged well above the average for my services. The training courses we run are the most personal, in-depth and dedicated around and are reflected in their fee as a result. My management company is without question the best around, so I charge handsomely for that, and so we have the relative comparison

to service offered and income earned. If something is of high value to others it will, as a result, be valued or desired and it should be represented by price, I urge you to charge well or to pay well for any such service, after all, these days, service is something that eludes most businesses, except in their generic advertising material of course.

Ok, so we now have the first figure on our ever-increasing fee scale, £250.

The next stage is to inform the solicitor of the purchase and instruct them to act, attached to this are the conveyance fees.

These include but are not limited to, the legal aspects and all of the relevant searches or notifications right the way through to the land registry etc., the fee we are usually charged comes in at around £750.

We now have a nice round running total of £1,000, just for making two phone calls.

The next batch of fees come from the lender, now this does differ greatly from lender to lender, but my example here is by using a typical 'high street' lender which is who we used for this recent purchase. Mortgage companies do have a tendency to charge all sorts of 'we just feel like it' fees, but most of these are simply added on to the mortgage principally. The main cost is the mortgage arrangement fee which can range anywhere between free, a few hundred pounds through to a couple of thousand, but the mortgage rate and fixed term will often reflect this in turn. Like I say, however, this can be added to the mortgage in most cases, so it's not absorbed as an initial fee for use in our example. The one fee the lender does make you pay upfront is the valuation fee for the property, and because of this, we've added it to our running total for the demonstration. The lender generally employs their own valuer and if their valuation does not stack up against the agreed purchase price the lender will not offer the requested amount, but instead 75% of their valuation.

Since the lender knows you may not proceed with the mortgage and since they generally use independent surveyors, this is why you have to pay these costs up front. The fee you pay does vary slightly from lender to lender, but typically costs are around £350. I have had deals where this was free but like I mentioned before this will always be slightly reflected in the product you receive.

Our running total is now a modest £1,350 and if the valuer comes back with a really low valuation or the vendor has had an increased, 'too good to be true' offer during this point and pulled out of the sale, we stand to lose a good portion of this total. This is not me trying to scare you but rather the harsh reality of the possibilities within the industry, in essence, though this tends not to happen so breath out slowly.

The lender will require you to have buildings insurance in place before you complete the purchase. On a property like this, it will, providing there are no special circumstances surrounding the rebuild or risk come in at around £110. I generally use CIA insurance, this is for ease, and because I have found them to be very competitive over the years. I am pretty sure that I could get a better deal now if I shifted my entire portfolio to someone else, but I have no call to at present, they have provided excellent service over the years, so I stick to what I know in this instance. Word of caution here make sure you accurately reflect the rebuild cost, this can be found on the valuation report in most cases.

Our fees are now running at £1,460.

There are no more fees for services to pay now, but there is the small sum of the 25% purchase contribution to pay, in this case, it was £17,000.

I have already mentioned that the SDLT is now 3% higher for second home purchases but because there is no stamp duty on purchases less than £125,000 the fee here is a flat 3% of the £68,000 which is £2040. The fee to register this payment with the land registry office should have already been included on your solicitor's invoice.

All in then this property left me, along with my mortgage which is higher than their 75% contribution due to their 'we just feel like it' mortgage arrangement fee of £1200, out of pocket to the sum of £20,500.

So, there you have it go back over the sums, digest them, learn them, reflect and understand that buying a property comes with certain costs that you don't really want to include but really need to in order to accurately gauge a properties potential. Of course, you can reduce these fees a little by shopping around for a cheaper solicitor or broker, but my advice here is, if you need to try to save a few hundred pounds on something as big as purchasing a property, then maybe you are in the wrong industry. The few extra pounds are invested well here and can save you time and energy in the long run by choosing quality and trusted professionals over cheap and cheerful ones.

Just a quick note to mention that the buildings insurance is a reoccurring running cost that can be offset against your tax liability. In essence, what you've just invested is a relatively low sum of money being that you now benefit from having under your control a property worth more than three times that value.

As a recap, here is a quick overview of the associated fees

Broker fee	**£250**
Solicitors conveyance charge	**£750**
Mortgage valuation fee	**£350**
Building insurance	**£110**
Stamp duty	**£2040**
Mortgage contribution	**£17,000**
Total outlay	**£20,500**

Part 2 - Purchasing property
Chapter 5, The purchasing procedure.

This can be a real complicated conundrum in itself and on the whole, is really beyond your control for the best part, I don't think I have ever been through the same process twice with this, seriously, there seems to be, every time, with every lender, with every solicitor and with every sale, a different approach.

The fundamentals ARE always the same however and using the same solicitor does help, especially when they are aware how you like things to be done. In some instances though It may not be as easy as using the same solicitor, we have 4 solicitors acting for us for varying reasons, but in general, it usually comes down to the lenders stipulation.

I will try to be brief here as it really won't teach you much except maybe how not to tear your hair out with every little request, fuss or demand the lender makes. I recently had to fill out a 19 page summary of a property I was selling, indicating all the locations of meters, stopcocks, boundaries, what we were leaving in the property, condition reports etc., fair right? Yes, I completely agree that protocol has to be adhered too. However, I was selling the property to myself to my own limited company or SPV, oh and there were three properties so yes three forms to fill in. The solicitors who were acting for the sale were the same solicitors who were acting for the purchase, they were just a separate branch, but they couldn't even agree on this. You can imagine how frustrated I was having to fill out 57 pages of pointless information, informing myself of things I already knew. It goes without saying I never reviewed the forms when they were included in my purchase pack, even though I could have written anything since I tried to get through them as fast as I could, and most probably slower than I got through the bottle of wine I had with me at the time. I have to say that was one of the most painful things I've ever had to do, and I've been for two endoscopies and a colonoscopy in the past three years, ouch!

You can pretty much gauge the purchase process from the information relating to the fees in the last chapter but, simplified the purchase process goes a little like this.

1) After viewing the property, the agent calls you, and you make an offer on the property.
2) The agent will require some proof of funds and in some cases a mortgage offer in principle from the lender in order to put the offer forward, in most cases however the proof of funds will be all that is needed and as you progress this may even become redundant.
3) You provide the proof of funds and explain that the mortgage request has been actioned and the offer in principle will follow; this will in 99% of cases be acceptable.

4) The offer is accepted by the vendor.
5) You inform your solicitor of the purchase and instruct them to act on your behalf.
6) After informing the agent on your choice of solicitor, they will issue that solicitor with the sale memorandum.
7) You will arrange the mortgage that best suits your strategy with your broker.
8) The broker will arrange the mortgage but will require a plethora of information from you, things like, but not limited to. Passport, driving licence, utility bills, three months bank statements, financial information relating to incomings and outgoings including other mortgages, details of any loans, proof of funds and usually both of your inside leg measurements. It is always the best course of action before you proceed that you go and see a broker just to make sure you meet the criteria for lenders.
9) Your solicitor will require some funds to carry out searches.
10) The next stage is where it slows down somewhat, the conveyance stage, the solicitors talk with each other, make sure that they have collected all the info relating to covenants, boundaries, building regulations for improvements, the right of way, drainage etc.
11) While this is going on the mortgage company will request payment for the valuation.

12) If this comes back in your favour, then the mortgage company will release the mortgage offer including any major stipulations or conditions.

13) Your solicitor and broker will check this through for you.

14) You will at this point need to arrange building insurance. Most lenders will not release their funds until they have been given proof of this, so once this is arranged, you should send a copy of the certificate to your solicitor.

15) A couple of days before the exchange of contracts it is a good idea to ask to view the property, this is to ensure that all the furniture, goods and rubbish have either been removed or left as discussed.

16) A final statement will arrive from your solicitor showing the amount you must transfer to complete the purchase; this will include the stamp duty contribution.

17) You will now transfer these funds into the solicitor's client account; It is at this point that contracts are usually exchanged, and the solicitor releases all the funds to the seller, including the lender's contribution & completion of sale takes place. This can be separated so that contracts are exchanged beforehand, but in my experience, this usually happens together and on the same day.

18) Next comes the phone call you have been waiting for, the call from the agent that tells you the keys are ready to collect. In my

experience, this comes about 2 hours after the call from my solicitor informing me that all is processed and that I should be able to collect the keys from the agent.

19) You now pick the keys up from the agent's office, and the real work begins.

Part 3 - letting and managing the property

Chapter 1, The first step

So, It's finally happened, all that talking, planning and action has become a reality, did you ever really think that this was going to happen?

You now own your very first investment property. The keys are in hand, the excitement is uncontrollably coursing through your veins, these feelings may be rapidly replaced by worry, nervousness and anxiety.

Perhaps now have the overwhelming task of getting the property ready for the rental market and the difficult task of finding that perfect tenant.

Oh, no, will anyone like it, will it sit on the market for months on end, will there be any major problems that you didn't notice on the viewing, why did no one else buy the property, was this really a good purchase or investment.

What if the tenants don't pay their rent or move on after trashing the place after only a few short months.

Ok, calm down, trust me when I tell you, we've all been there, if you've done your research well used careful due diligence, followed the sound advice within this book, maybe trained with us or had some sound mentorship from an experienced investor then you have done your very best to avoid any major problems arising.

So, what do you do now?

Well, before I answer this question, I would like to make a very important point.

One of the most important things to remember when assessing the work that is required to bring the property up to a rentable standard is; **The overall condition of your property will ultimately reflect the type of tenant it houses**.

If your property is barely habitable or falling apart at the seams or even just a bit tatty or smelly, then your tenants get to pick you or the property.

Conversely, if your property has a lovely inviting feel, its clean, tidy, warm and in good order then you get to pick your tenants, it goes without saying that the latter is the desired outcome.

I always ask two fundamental questions here.

1) Why would someone want to live in this property
2) Why would they want to leave this property

I feel these two fundamental questions really speak for themselves and require no elaboration.

So, what do you do now?

Well, I always, and I mean always, drive straight to the property.
I want to get a very clear perspective of exactly what the property actually requires now that all the furniture is removed, the pictures

and rugs have been taken, and the grass hasn't been cut in the last eight or so weeks.

When I enter the property, I take care to note how the property smells, everyone has different sensitivities to smell but generally, if you can smell damp, dogs, cats etc. so can the prospective tenants.
If it smells clean great, if not I note it down on my pad to action as soon as is reasonably practicable
I do, however, always have a boot full of plug-in air fresheners, these can be purchased for £2 from stores like Aldi and can be refilled for £1 thereafter.

I then have a brief walk around the property in its entirety gauging the overall feel of the place, I note the gas and electric meter readings, and if there is a water meter, I take that reading down also.
I fire up the heating and adjust the clock so that it comes on for two hours in the morning, an hour in the afternoon and two hours in the evening at around 17 degrees; this helps the heating tick over but most importantly prevents the property from losing its residual heat.
There is nothing worse than walking into a property that is cold to its core, it's depressing and will slow any process of assessment or work down as you won't want to be there or at best will want to be somewhere else rather quickly.
I would seasonally turn the cold water stop tap off also. Contrary to popular misconceptions this will not affect the heating in any way.

Next, I will walk through each room individually, checking light bulbs, light switches, door operation and noting down any necessary repairs in one column on my pad. In the other column goes the 'possible' repairs or required upgrades like carpets, painting, blinds etc.

Once I have compiled my list, I usually take photos, these are very handy when properties are to be renovated.

Having before and after photos are great to use as evidence when a valuer turns up for their revaluation assessment six months after purchase.

These photos can save time and energy trying to convince them that a property that was valued at £65,000, six months ago is now worth £90,000. I generally have a to-let board ready to install on my initial visit, and I also try to catch the neighbours where possible, most of the time the neighbours will be trying to catch you anyway, so it's not that hard.

The purpose here is to inform the neighbour that this will be a rented property, but to dispel any doubts they may have.

I let them know that it's my clear intention to house good, trustworthy tenants.

This, hopefully, stops the neighbours worrying and affirming their initial negative thoughts through auto-suggestion that the place is going to become a stereotypical doss house which is generally their initial reaction if you don't speak with them before the board goes up.

People will typically think the worst about us landlords due to the bad press we get, remember we are all modern-day scrooges according to the masses. To nip this in the bud early on without the neighbours having time for their worst-case scenarios to manifest and subsequently take hold I think is very important.

I do have a small favour to ask you here.

Please, as a way of thanking me for the hours laboured writing this book always offer me the one following courtesy.

Please, please, please always install a professional to-let board and not a handmade board or a poster in the window, even purchasing a one-off board is inexpensive and can be worth its weight in gold.
They just create the right message or offer the desired impression of you as a landlord.

Hand or homemade boards, window posters just scream rouge landlord, they scream tight landlord, they scream half arsed landlord, they scream unprofessional landlord, and they just help to fuel the fire of the publics general perception of landlords as a whole. Furthermore, the prospective tenants know this, and instead of attracting the nice hard working family type tenants who intend on making your property a home you will attract the kind of tenant who can sense the cracks that are already appearing in your strategy.

These undesirable tenants will pray on you like you wouldn't believe, the lack of care for the property is obvious to them, and they seek these types of landlords out consciously, but more about that later.

The next thing I do at this stage is to advertise the property through the chosen portals and organise the necessary repairs or refurbishments from my list and if required the full renovation.
I won't patronize you here by telling you to get fixed quotes from at least two reputable companies, find people you trust that have in the best case, been recommended to you that can offer sound advice and solutions to your problems and fundamentally get their timescales on email or written down as proof. You may not be experienced property investors yet but I can imagine that you're not stupid either and in a roundabout way I got to say what I wanted by offering mitigation initially. Win, win.

Part 3 - letting and managing the property

Chapter 2, Where to advertise and at what price

Before we delve into this section here is a quick overview of the process of advertising your property some of the list, in particular, the ones relating to fees, epc's etc. are mandatory requirements and can carry hefty fines if not adhered to.

1) Advertise the property through your chosen portals; to-let boards, Gumtree, Rightmove or Upad, local landlord sites, Facebook groups, local papers, personal websites, twitter feeds etc.

2) Include in the description the EPC, price of the property per month or week, the information on the required bond, all the relevant costs including any administration fees and include details of your application process, these, as well as being a mandatory requirement with the exception of the application process description, help to portray the correct image to good honest tenants as well as acting as a deterrent to the other less desirable kind.

3) Include as many glowing pictures of the property as possible including externals, front and rear.

4) Provide an email address for people to contact you electronically as well as any other chosen method, people are losing the confidence of face to face or verbal communication through the

rise of anti-social media so as a result, email or text contact is becoming increasingly common.

5) If providing a mobile number, clearly state the contact hours. It's surprising how many texts or calls our company mobile gets after 9pm, we've had missed calls at 1am with answer phone messages asking for details on a particular property, it may not surprise you to hear that we never returned the call. Often these inappropriately timed messages will start with "I'm sorry it's late but" as if that mitigates the rudeness of it somehow, remember not all of these are aware that we are an agency.

6) Perhaps provide a link to a more in-depth advert, for example, a link to your advert on another site if relevant.

7) Provide any information on the type of tenant you are looking for, e.g. working tenants preferred, DSS accepted, no pets allowed children welcome etc., it's your property so feel free to let to whomever you choose but be careful not to be prejudice or discriminative towards anyone.

The more information you can put on your advert the better as it cuts down wasted time dealing with the types of tenants you are evidentially trying to avoid and increases the probability of receiving a call from the tenants you are trying to source.

I am assuming that all your repairs, refurbishment or renovations are now either, arranged in principle, well under way or fully completed.

If you are going to renovate the property fully you need to gauge the timeframe accurately, so that you don't advertise the property online too early. You will be too far down the listings when its ready to let if you are advancing on a three-month renovation timeframe.

Most sites only advertise properties for a specified duration, i.e. three months, so ideally you want to advertise the property when all the installations are finishing so the tenant can fully visualise the end results of the property.

I generally advertise the property when it is about four weeks from completion. Most tenants will need to offer around four weeks' notice to their current landlord or agent anyway, so this will tie in nicely with your timescale.

If there are only minor cosmetics to carry out, then the property should be advertised through your chosen portals without delay. We have already discussed putting up a board on your initial inspection of the property, and I do this whether the property is to be fully renovated or not, it creates interest and the more people who see the board, the better.

I always place my properties on Gumtree and some other local sites, including of course our own website initially. I find, because of the level of the property we deal with I yield better results from sites like Gumtree than I do from the likes of Rightmove or other such portals.

Sometimes where necessary, we will upload the properties through a site called Upad, this, in turn, adds them to Rightmove, Zoopla and the likes for around £120 per listing and is well worth it for the exposure it generates.

The price you decide to advertise and ultimately let the property at should have been looked at already when researching your strategy or at least when researching the properties potential before purchasing. However, this may have changed for many reasons or just been worked out as a roundabout figure initially. There really is no right or wrong answer here except that it should fit your strategy and financial standing.

Although it may indeed help, don't be fooled into thinking that keeping your rent low will keep your tenants at the property for longer or, conversely by raising your rent annually will they feel the need to leave.
You want value for your property and to achieve the desired return, but it is my opinion that you shouldn't try to squeeze every penny out of your tenant either, especially with the initial let.
Tenants often underestimate the costs associated with renting or their ability to manage such costs; your tenant may be left short every week or month, reducing their quality of life and subsequent attitude towards their rented property and paying their rent.

Remember you will have to go a long way to find a tenant that will treat your property like a home but if you are able to find one your strategy should be that of maintaining the current relationship or status of that tenancy.

My advice here is always the same, don't be desperate, don't rush the let by dropping the price after a few weeks as this again can give the wrong impression.

Try not to be too greedy and overprice the property either as this may mean that you price yourself out of finding a suitable tenant, it may again sound like another get out of jail free card, but I would and generally do price my properties at the same price as others price their like for like properties in the area. This I feel creates a level playing field for everyone but more importantly because my properties tend to be of a higher standard it persuades the best tenants to come across to us, and the resulting factor means they have no controllable reason to leave, remember my two questions from earlier, why would someone want to rent and why would they want to leave.

The most important thing here is to pick your tenants carefully. Having a good tenant occupy your property can really alleviate all the stresses from being a landlord but conversely having a 'nightmare' tenant occupy your property can compound them.

In my opinion, this is one of the hardest aspects of property investing and its the one that over 75% of investors get completely wrong.

Never fear, however, I have become an expert in letting and I intend on sharing my knowledge and expertise with you.

Our biggest asset within our management company or our unique selling point (USP) is the fact that we have the ability to match the best tenants possible for the property the investor provides us with. Whether that's a £50,000 dated ex-council estate property or a £200,000 modernised detached village property we can always find a suitable, reliable tenant for the property.

I will run through our rigorous process with you so that you can share in my knowledge and wisdom of suitable tenant finding. My only hope here is that none of the landlords or agents in my local area read this book.

Section 3 - letting and managing the property
Chapter 3, Finding and vetting a tenant

The property is advertised through your chosen means; your professional looking board is erected generating interest and raising awareness for the passing trade as well as the local residents.

You will now most certainly start to get calls about your property.

As I explained on the last page, you have now entered the hardest part of being a property investor. It's relatively easy and often fun sourcing and viewing properties. It's very exciting negotiating a price that suits you and your chosen strategy or budget, and it can be thrilling as it makes you feel important or progressive talking things through with your broker or solicitor.

The renovation process can be challenging but incredibly satisfying watching the whole process slot together like a carefully planned jigsaw, but now the reality has to set in.

Your property is to become someone else' home; your job so far is done. The process of finding a tenant now takes a different turn, it requires a completely different thought process or approach, and It should be treated with the highest regard.

I see so many landlords failing at this very crucial stage, in essence, this is the entire industry summed up in one simple action.

I don't care how great the property is, what price you paid or how modern the interior is, the industry is based on the tenant and their longevity.

Most landlords go through the whole process of sourcing, buying and renovating with great care only to let the property to the first tenant that shows an interest or hands this over to an agent that only cares if the tenant passes their generic paper exercise test.

Clean criminal record and low adverse credit history? You're in! Don't get me wrong these landlords and agents are a godsend to me, these landlords give the poor tenants somewhere to live, keeping the right kind of tenant for me.

Without these impatient and overzealous landlords, my job would be a whole lot harder since I would have to sift more diligently.

These are also the very same landlords who give my management company more business each year since they realise, they can't manage their properties like they thought they could.

The irony is, however, they can, they just pick the wrong kind of tenants due to their haste, lack of understanding of the principles and unwillingness to change.

Perhaps, one day in our training room would save them thousands in management fees over the course of their mortgage term, a small price to pay to gain the insight from years of experience.

These landlords are also the source of most of the negative comments that surround the industry, comments like "oh it's a nightmare" or "the last tenant I had was a right one" people are always asking me "isn't it a nightmare dealing with problem tenants" or "don't you have problems with people trashing your properties all the time".

Without these comments or general negative attitudes, the industry may be swamped with wanna be investors and subsequently overran with cheap rental properties.

Every time someone asks me about a so-called 'nightmare' tenant, my answer is always "no not really".

I tend not to go into any depth; I don't feel the need to educate them or waste time trying to change their already distorted opinions.

People will always believe what they want to believe, and generally, that's the worst-case scenario, who am I to break their misinformed illusions.

Bearing in mind that the mathematics, that of the laws of averages are firmly stacked against me due to the number of properties we are now responsible for within our own portfolio and through our management company, we have been extremely successful in finding reliable tenants.

It all comes down to our ability to choose the right tenant carefully and to show patience in the quest for them initially.

In the same way I urged you to be patient in the pursuit for a property I urge you to be the same in the quest for a tenant, they may not come along right away, but the right tenant will always come along eventually.

The patience we apply is where our success lies, we don't feel the need to immediately fill our properties with a questionable tenant, and we don't get worried when they don't let in the first week or two of advertising.

We are continually educating our landlords and reminding them of the famous Guinness advert, that 'good things come to those who wait'. Why put months and months of hard work into a project coupled with many thousands of pounds to have it all unravel like a well-plotted Tarantino movie just because you couldn't wait a few extra weeks for the right kind of tenant to come along at an approximate cost saving of £150.

Would you save for a lifetime to buy your dream Ferrari and then let your 17-year-old son take it on a road trip to Newquay with his friends? No! Why? Because you know that he and perhaps more so, his friends would not look after it in the way you would want it to be looked after, and the same applies here in your search for a tenant.

Ok so how do you find the right tenant?

Well, the first point has already been explained, and that is to adopt patience, I'm not saying that this will definitely take a long time and that the right tenant won't come along on the first viewing, but the underlying point is that if they don't, don't let desperation lead you to compromise.

If you have any reservations at all, then it is always best to air on the side of caution and be assured by my experience that the right tenant will eventually come along.

If you've got a nice looking property that's clean and tidy, then trust me when I say that someone will come along that will appreciate this in the way you want them to.

You have, at this point spent, in most cases tens of thousands of pounds on the property, so a few extra hundred in council tax and mortgage payments won't make any real difference in the long term. Being hasty in your choice of a tenant can lead to many more thousands of pounds wasted in damage or rental arrears.

Remember that this small loss is against your tax liability anyway.

The next thing I advise you to do and this is something we always do but yet I am still to see or meet anyone else who does this is to pre-vet the tenants before they view the property. This is done with a pre-viewing questionnaire, this is not a lengthy, arduous questionnaire but rather a quick gauge of their current situation but more importantly, it is to act as a pre-filter and deterrent to the kind of tenants you simply don't want to rent your property.

The questionnaire is a data input form on our website; we just direct prospective tenants there through a link sent to their email address or mobile phone number depending on how they contacted us initially. You could send these questions in a text message but don't verbally ask the questions over the phone, this is what others do, and it is where they fail. We used to send these via text years ago, but due to the high volume of inquiries we now receive we had to systemize the process.

As mentioned, it is essential that these questions are not simply asked on the phone, the trick here is to call them to action, it helps gauge the tenant's effort levels and to filter the undesirable tenants.

Our form is sent via a link to email or text, and I would estimate that we do not get a response to 50% of these.

Either they can't be bothered to click on the link and fill in the drop box blanks, or more accurately they know that they do not fit our criteria. Either way, we win, not only do they fail to apply we haven't had our time wasted by showing the property to a tenant that we would never consider an application from anyway.

Now, by asking these questions verbally over the phone you may get some distorted version of the truth, or the tenant may try to pull the wool over your eyes completely, but by calling them to take action, they are wasting their own time by filling in a form when they know they have something to hide. Nine times out of ten if they have something to hide they will just move on to the next unsuspecting landlord, result right? Well not for the next landlord it isn't.

We currently ask the following question.

1) The address of the property they wish to view
2) Their full name
3) Email address
4) Mobile number
5) Dob
6) Current address
7) Current landlord or agent
8) Would they be able to obtain a reference from their current landlord or agent
9) Their reason for moving home
10) How long have they been at their current address for
11) How is the rent to be paid – working tenant, benefit, mix of both
12) Any serious credit issues
13) Any County Court Judgements

Yes, the observant readers will have noted that the above is another anti superstitious 13-point list. You can see by now that I am not a superstitious person, I am instead one who has beliefs in science rather than that of the supernatural.

You can also see from the above list that in general we only require a small amount of information but what we can gauge from these details is staggering, not only from the information obtained but in the way they either answer them or rather more accurately don't answer them.

There are particular types of tenants, the ones you don't want to occupy your property which will only want to rent from a private unsuspecting landlord, they won't or rather can't approach letting agents or landlords who are thorough in their vetting. You don't want to be this type of landlord, but rather the type of landlord that these tenants avoid.

By setting up the pre-questionnaire, you are setting yourself up for the best possible outcome initially. Any tenant who has anything to hide, who is doing a moonlight flit, who has a history of not paying their rent, who has been evicted or is currently being evicted will either not give these answers, or they will be that unconvincing that it will stand out like a sore thumb. Conversely, you know that the tenants that have nothing to hide will fill the form in completely. And the tenants who don't have anything to hide, but still can't be bothered to fill the form in? Well, do you really want a tenant like that, someone who can't be bothered to fill in a 3-minute form to rent a property for themselves or their family?

The answer to that question is no, in case you're confused.

You can now gauge how the tenant responds to the requested questions on the form.

Will they give one word hard to decipher answers or will they be concise and clear, will they answer the questionnaire immediately or two days later, after other viewings haven't gone their way. Will they give you a version of war and peace in their reason for moving, citing that their last landlord is X Y & Z and that the property is this, that or the other.

These are all signs that reflect their personality and should be duly noted.

It goes without saying that someone who returns the form immediately with clear, concise information not only has nothing to hide but is a good communicator also. This is possibly the tenant you are looking for. You see by asking the questions you already have a rough idea of the tenant you are going to meet and show your property to; it saves so much wasted time and possible wool pulling by clever, manipulative tenants.

Like I've just said, on average only 50% of people who contact us about a property actually fill in this form, but of that 50%, we rent to approximately 80% thereafter.

Without the questionnaire, you are susceptible to the prospective tenant's mind games and possible 'little white lies' on the viewing. You will hear every line in the book over the coming years. Tenants have always either just re-decorated or fitted carpets throughout their current property, completely at their own expense, of course; they are only moving because the landlord won't repair the boiler or because there is damp throughout the property and they need to move as its affecting the children's asthma.

Although these stories may have some element of truth or in fact be entirely true, please air on the side of caution, you may be a trusting, honest, kind and decent person but in this industry, you need to adapt quickly, or this will be abused and leveraged by predatory tenants.

Trust is something that needs to be earned within the property industry, a tenant has to earn this by action, not by words, trust in this industry it is not unconditional, and you need to treat every tenant in the same way initially, by treading with small, cautious and wary steps.

By using our previewing questionnaire or as we call it the 'wasted time saving' questionnaire it prevents us from turning up to a viewing on one of our nice newly renovated properties only to be met by an undesirable tenant. The young couple wearing tracksuits and baseball caps, two kids in a pushchair, one of whom is eating a Greggs pasty and the other eating a packet of cheesy hula hoops. Of course, they've brought their friends with them who don't seem to be able to grasp the basic concept of the English language let alone hold down a coherent conversation. The first question they ask you is "do you accept pets" because they have 2 Staffordshire bull terriers, of course, they call them Staffies. This question is swiftly followed up by "can we pay the bond in instalments and do you need a guarantor"?

Ok so I have tried to be as stereotypical as I can here, but this can and sometimes does happen, with the form you stand the best possible chance of avoiding such viewings

By the way, I have nothing against Staffordshire bull terriers; they can be and often are lovely natured dogs in the right hands, it is the stereotypical types who own them I don't like.

Ok so now you have the previewing questionnaire you can eliminate the above scenario, well mostly anyway.
I always find it odd when speaking with landlords who don't find the basic information out before a viewing; they are walking into the unknown, seemingly clinging to the hope that this tenant will be the one.
They often carry on with this in typical 'head burying' fashion by letting to the tenants that I've just stereotyped above.
They seem to wonder where it all went wrong and why they are the ones that are always 'unlucky' with tenants.
If I am going to reiterate another point over and over again until it sticks like glue, it's the point of having patience within the industry and by choosing a good tenant in the right time-frame, not as fast as you can in order to bring yourself a singular moment of comfort.
Surely we all know the benefits of delayed gratification by now.
Next comes the viewing, the moment where you get to see the face behind the form. This is the point where perhaps you have to have a certain detachment.

The people you meet will reflect the area and value of your property. This is the point where you need to cut the prospective tenants a little slack as the saying goes.

These people are in rented accommodation, and for the best part, excluding a small percentage of the rented population and an even lower percentage of my reader's tenants, they will not have masses of disposable income.

Their entire makeup from here on in will reflect this. That said and accepted they should not be judged by this.

We have had, over the years hundreds of tenants who dress rather unappealing, don't seem to have much disposable income but who are very clean, polite and all in excellent tenants. Obviously, you still need to notice the signs that are presenting themselves overwhelmingly.

If their personal hygiene is well below par, or they smell heavily of smoke, and their car is overflowing with crisp packets, MacDonald's wrappers and coke cans when they pull up to meet you, this is a reflection of their personality and cleanliness and should be noted.

You don't need to have surplus income to shower or use a bin. You will have by now, already worked out what kind of tenant you are looking for.

This is something I will not offer any advice on since I do not want to be prejudice against anyone, but also I don't want to be a walking contradiction of my own selections.

We have every tenant under the sun. Young single mum's on benefits with four children. Tenants with two dogs and a pet snake. Young brothers living together in their first home since they have just fled the nest. Old retired couples who have sold their home to move into rented accommodation to utilise their assets money for quality of life. We have tenants renting a three bedroom property with no children but five cats. Tenants in high paid jobs living in single room accommodation, tenants who have split from their partners which generally suggests short-term tenancies but have been with us for five years plus. Foreign tenants, predominantly from Eastern Europe who work three jobs for about 4000 hours per week to send as much money home to the family as possible and even tenants who have previously been homeless for a short period, usually sleeping on their friend's couch for a few months until their friend gets a little sick of them. These tenants are from every walk of life and from different backgrounds and completely different life stories, but the one thing they all have in common is that they passed our rigours testing and vetting. They are all good, desirable tenants who look after the property as if were their own home and fundamentally pay their rent on time each month.

It is up to you to decide what your preferences are regarding the selection of a suitable tenant, if any, and which tenants you will not rent to. Remember that there are currently no laws to state that you can or cannot choose any particular type of tenant. If you want to choose eastern Europeans because of their ethics in paying their rent as a priority or you don't want to rent to anyone under the age of 30 then this is entirely up to you, no one can govern this or influence this. You may want to rent to working tenants only or to DSS tenants only since you know that the rent is almost guaranteed from the local council, whatever you decide is up to you.

The small piece of advice I will offer here is to have an open mind. If they pass the tests, you place in front of them then why not?

Ok, so back to the viewing.

Remember earlier in the book when I told you that I get to a property viewing around 30 minutes before, so I can check the area out.

But also so I can catch the agent out trying to light the property, remove the junk mail, put the heating on etc. Well, guess what, those tricks are great. I fully advise you to apply them on your showings, and I will give you some advice on dressing the property in a moment.

When you visit the property for the showing, get there 20-30 minutes early at least, take some air freshener with you and open all the windows as well as the front and back doors for a few minutes. Walk through the property and blast each room with a good but not to heavy spray of air freshener turning on ALL lights as you go including any extraction and any under-counter lights. I don't care if it's late at night or the sunniest day of the year, lights always give the property a warm and inviting feeling. Next, unless its summer you want to put the heating on to warm the property to a nice comfortable temperature, if this is a particularly cold, windy or unpleasant day then nice and warm is around 21 degrees otherwise 18/19 degrees will suffice. You are now ready to welcome what could be your next long-term tenant, but before we get there, I will walk you through a few things we do to dress a property before we show it.

We always place a long carpet runner or the longest possible that space allows, at the front door. This does three things; the obvious one is that it primarily prevents any wet or muddy feet marking the carpets or flooring. The second benefit is that it demonstrates to the tenant that we like a clean property and that we expect the flooring to be looked after. The final thing it does is to add a splash of colour to what is most likely a very neutral room with a covering of cream, magnolia, white or light grey walls and beige or grey carpets.

A small rug in the living room and colourful bath mats in the bathroom is always a good idea too. This again adds a splash of colour and a sign of comfort to the rooms. Another thing we generally do is to hang pictures and mirrors throughout the property; we don't overdo this, we simply place these in and around the property where we feel they are needed. if there is a fireplace, we will often just stand a large wooden mirror on the mantel.

We will place a couple of large pictures on the walls in the living room, maybe one or two in the kitchen and a few in the bedrooms or up the stairs if space permits.

Any area we feel is large dead wall space or has a particular cold feel will be filled. We often put a tea, coffee, and sugar set out along with a kettle and a plastic sink bowl and maybe a glass or wood chopping board by the sink.

The bathroom always has, along with the previously mentioned floor mats, a toilet brush, hand towel and if possible, a candle display on the windowsill or shelf.

The one thing all these items have in common is colour; we generally stick to the same colour scheme through the property, it, along with the lights and heating gives the property a nice warm, inviting and cosy feel.

This attention to detail will be something that will appeal to your tenant, consciously or sub-consciously.

The other advantage here is that it gives a sense of what the property can look like furnished and prevents the property from looking drab and cold or better explained as undesirable.

Many people fail to see past the emptiness of a cold and unfurnished property, so it is your job here to demonstrate it's potential.

The tenant is now at your front door; you're both about to make your first impressions. Are they early or late, if they are late do they have an excuse and is it plausible? Do they even mention that they are late? How are they dressed, how do they introduce themselves.

Do they remove their shoes? Are their shoes clean, this is not a job interview I hear you say, and although you are quite right you must realise that their actions are demonstrations of their personality, they are providing you with information with every action. If they don't take their muddy shoes off when you are presenting the house to them for the first time, then it's safe to assume this will never happen.

If you know what you are looking for there is an opportunity to gain an overall picture of your tenant at every juncture, even before they have finished viewing the property, just take note of all the signs.

How you introduce yourself to them is equally important, you must come across as a knowledgeable and professional landlord. You must never give them the impression that this is your first time. Adopt this professional and knowledgeable approach from the very first moment. You must lay down the gauntlet and command their respect immediately; you must set a precedence that is there to follow throughout the tenancy.

Remember they are there to impress you in their eyes, although you do need to be aware that subconsciously they are judging you at the same time.

There is always plenty of time, later on, to develop a somewhat personal relationship if you so desire. Your prospective tenant will now walk through the property; I often let them just get on with this as they see fit, I loosely follow them and observe their behaviour, don't stray too far away from them that they can't ask you questions if needed but don't stay too close that they don't talk amongst themselves. You want to be able to hear their conversations clearly to gauge an idea of their intentions and thoughts on the property which will aid in the feedback and the overall picture building of the possible tenants.

The questions that a tenant asks on a viewing can be as random as the drop of the lottery balls on a Saturday night, but it is very important that you have all the fundamental answers to the basic questions that may be asked.

Questions relating to the council tax rates, gas and electric supplier, if the meters are contracted or card meters, local bin collections and if there are any water meters present are all fundamental.

Often tenants will ask on the viewing if you accept pets, and if this is not your desire, then it may be best if you incorporate this into your pre-viewing questionnaire or respective advertising to reduce the possibilities of time-wasted viewings.

Let's assume that all in all the tenant seems to fit the property and the area it is in, you get a decent enough impression of their intentions, and they inform you that they want to rent the property.

The next thing we do is let them know how our application process works; we also remind them of the administration fee that is attached to the application. I say remind as the tenants should already be aware of this since it is a legal requirement when advertising a property that all fees attached to renting the property are to be highlighted in the advert initially.

The reason we have an application is to gain further insight into the tenant's personality and also to gather crucial information in order to complete our security, right to rent and credit checks further.
The reason we charge an administration fee and why I am so against the government from taking this right away from landlords is not so that we have another revenue stream but rather, again to act as a deterrent to possible rouge tenants and also so that the tenants are truthful on their application.

We currently only charge £69.99 for our single person administration fee and £99.99 for a joint application fee, this is a small enough amount that it does not really phase the tenants, but it is large enough that they do not want to lose their money either by giving fraudulent or inaccurate information on their application.

Our pre-viewing questionnaire is designed to put off the wrong kind of tenants, but we have found that some tenants tell little white lies on this questionnaire to get their foot in the door. Every so often a deceitful tenant gets through to the viewing stage, but it is at the application stage where this deceit ends.

All prospective tenants are made aware that the fee is non-refundable, and if they are not 100% truthful, they will fail the application and subsequently lose their fee.
How many deceitful tenants that have managed to get to the viewing stage will then continue to the application stage?
guessed it in one, NONE!

The application form is never given to the tenant on the viewing; our application is currently a five-page form and almost every tenant who views a property will take the form if you have it with you. This is human nature, people will either take it to be polite as they don't have either the ability or confidence to let you know they are not interested in renting the property or they will intend on filling it in only to decide later that day that they didn't like the property as much as they thought they did, once the dust has settled.
You are then left suspended in animation for several days wondering if they are going to return the form. Several days pass, so you contact them only to find out that they have been accepted into a different property or worse they just ignore your approach completely. What's worse is you had a really great feeling about them, your naivety let you believe they were going to complete the form, so you foolishly put a hold on all other viewings.

By not handing the form out on a viewing it removes most of the guesswork, but it also saves time and energy contemplating or second-guessing others actions. Oh and it saves on paper and ink also, the more properties you have, believe me, you will get sick of printing and giving these applications out on every viewing.
Sometimes we show the same property four or five times in one day, that's a lot of wasted paper.

If the prospective tenants really like the property and indicate their intentions to continue through to the application process, we tell them to go away and think about it. We ask them to have a lengthy discussion, and if they still decide they want to continue through to the application stage, they are to send us their email address or to confirm via email if we already have this. It is at this point we will forward the form electronically and be rather confident that we have in fact found our tenant, this is of course if we choose to continue in this process ourselves. Just because an application has been requested doesn't always mean it will be supplied. This delay in a request for an application gives the option to the prospective tenant to pull out if that was their true intention anyway, cool off if they got a little carried away with the viewing but mostly and more importantly it lets them talk themselves into really wanting the property. This is the desired result as it shifts all the leverage over to you as the landlord. It also gives us a chance to digest the viewing and decide if we would like to provide them with an application.

The application form should be sent directly to their email address. Tenants who have no email address, access to printers or no internet access are really either undesirable or un-resourceful. Either way, they are not who you want to rent to.

We are in an age where people have access to this kind of technology through their watches and can turn on lights or their TV's through voice command, so if someone doesn't have access to either of the above, I do question his or her life choices and tend not to want any further part in them.

We do not process this form until the funds are received in full, it demonstrates their commitment and shows their initial financial status, someone who has to wait a week for the application fee may again not be the most desirable applicant. We usually only give 72 hours to return both the form and the fee, or we tend to terminate the application, this is of course unless a longer timeframe has been previously agreed either at the viewing stage or upon receiving the application request.

We used to suspend viewings at this stage because we saw it as potentially wasted time, but something I advise everyone to do is to continue advertising and booking out viewings at this stage.

If the application isn't successful, or the applicants don't return the completed application form for any reason, then it is time wasted and possibly a suitable missed tenant.

We will stress to all the tenants from here on in that we have already released an application so we cannot release another until we are in a position to do so, i.e. the pending application fails or is terminated by either party.

How you produce your application is up to you, but our application form has all the usual collective information such as name, address, D.O.B's, National insurance number, previous addresses, contact information, employment details, work and landlord references, we again ask them for credit information and also CCJ information.
I know some agents that won't release their application without the fee being paid, this is, as they see it for compensation for the wasted time if the tenant has CCJ's or any other misdemeanours that will prevent the tenancy from materialising.

Along with the generic information on the application, we also include a list of questions we feel are relevant to gauge how long we think the tenancy is going to last for.
For example, are they looking for a short term or long term tenancy? Our questions are geared up to decipher this information without them knowing, we do ask this basic question outright, and often we are told that they want a long-term tenancy, but then the other answers we receive seem to contradict this.
The questions we ask on the application gives us insight to determine the real answers we desire.

We also, from our questions try to gauge the tenant's intentions while in the property and can often obtain an overall view of their personality and therefore suitability from this. Again, the application form makes up part of our training courses and is supplied to you so that you can either use as it is or extract and edit as you see fit.

Just visit www.wiseowlpropertytraining.co.uk

Section 3 - letting and managing the property
Chapter 4, Setting up the tenancy

So Your tenant has produced what can only be described as the perfect application. They want a long-term tenancy, they have agreed the rental amount, and have their deposit in full. All their personal information checks out, and the references from their workplace and previous landlords have all come back in glowing fashion. Their credit score is impeccable, and they have no outstanding county court judgements.

It is now time to set their tenancy up, however, these days, doing this may be harder than you realise.

To prevent problems further down the line, there are many things that need to be done here and to be done right; this is why agents charge so much for tenant finding fees.

As regulations continually change and are ever evolving it is your responsibility to find out the current regulations for signing up and maintaining a tenancy. My advice here is to join the National Landlords Association or Residential Landlords Association along with any local landlord associations that may be in your local investment or area of residence.

These associations can be invaluable in terms of advice or information sharing; some local landlord associations even have tenant referencing whereby existing landlords will give their feedback on past tenants, this can be a huge asset at your previewing questionnaire stage and can save a lot of wasted time and energy when a tenant flags up on the 'unwanted' list.

Setting up a tenancy used to be a relatively straightforward task, almost as simple as giving out a contract or AST but these days in a world gone mad the process is a slightly more complex one and can carry hefty fines if not adhered to correctly.

In order to set up a tenancy, I do the following, and most of these are mandatory requirements in England and Wales.
My advice is to research well, speak with the NLA or RLA and follow these steps as a guideline at the time of printing only:

1) You must give the tenants an AST (Assured Shorthold Tenancy Agreement), you can print these off the NLA or RLA's website for a fee or for free once you are a member, but another good site for tenancy documentation and a great little book to read is Landlord Law by Tessa Shepperson, see www.landlordlaw.co.uk.

2) You must check that the tenants have the right to rent in the UK, you can find details on this at www.gov.uk/check-tenant-right-to-rent-documents.

3) You must provide your tenant with a copy of the how to rent guide booklet which can be found at www.gov.uk/goverment/publcations/how-to-rent.

4) You must provide information on Legionnaires' disease and demonstrate the purging by operating the water taps throughout the property in a well-ventilated room, preferably with the windows open and run these taps for at least 5 minutes. Some documentation or advice can be obtained at www.wiseowlproperty.co.uk/tenancysetup.

5) You must provide the tenant with a copy of the current gas safety inspection otherwise known as the CP12 gas safety certificate. Note here that this must be carried yearly or more accurately within a 12-month period of the last certificate.

6) You must provide and demonstrate to the tenant the correct operation of the smoke alarms; current regulations state that one per floor is required; we always place one in the hall and the other at the top of the stairs. Contrary to popular belief, these alarms do not need to be hard wired in single let properties.

7) **YOU MUST,** and for the listeners benefit here this information is written in block capitals and highlighted as bold text, protect the tenants' bond within a 30-day period of receiving it, even if they pay in increments. Along with this, you must also give the tenant the information of which Deposit Protection scheme is used, all the prescribed information and the guide on deposits which are all obtained from their website, incidentally we use the Deposit Protection Service or the DPS for this. It is a complete preference

which body you use of course as they all do what they say on the tin.

8) Although not a legal requirement it is a good idea to complete a full inventory and checklist otherwise known as a schedule of condition and content report, this should be backed up with photos and video evidence if possible. We carry out the inventory the day before the check-in, but the video is always carried out in the presence of the tenant, and we always get them to confirm the date in the video also.

9) Always document the electric and gas meter readings along with any water meter readings and have the tenant sign this form.

10) We always demonstrate the correct operation of the heating system, informing the tenant what to check if the boiler does not work. This usually starts with the gas meter and moves on to checking the pressure on a combination boiler whilst demonstrating how to reset and refill the appliance if necessary.

11) We always show the tenants the location of the stop tap and inform them that if there are any leaks they must turn this tap clockwise fully and open all taps to purge the system, this is fundamental information and can save thousands of pounds in the long run. It also stops the tenant calling you at 2am to tell you they have an uncontrollable leak.

12) It is wise to give the tenant some reliable information on condensation and the avoidance of resulting problems. One of the

most common problems reported to landlords is the problem of 'damp' this is a very loose term as nine times out of ten the problem is indeed condensation and nine out of those ten times the problem is often living conditions. The tenant is either not heating or ventilating the property sufficiently, or they are creating excess moisture either through cooking, showering or drying clothes on radiators. Giving the tenant some preventative information at the start of the tenancy can help to alleviate such problems. Again, we have all the advice on our website at www.wiseowlproperty.co.uk/tenancy-setup.

13) Make sure that the tenants are fully aware of their payment date and of what reference to use on the payment. A quick note here, if the tenant pays weekly, you must provide them with a rent card if possible, get the tenants to pay monthly or in the case of top-up payments four weekly so that they are in line with the benefit payments.

14) The next thing to do is to hand the tenant all of the information along with a set of keys and ideally a log book for the property with all the information included as well as any other information you think is relevant.

15) The final part of the equation is to inform the necessary utility companies and the local council of the change of tenancy and subsequent liability for the bills.

We have a checklist form that we use that covers all the above, and again it is available when attending any of our training courses.

In summary; You've bought your property at a good price, you've got it to a good rentable standard on a economical budget. You've found a fantastic tenant who is paying the desired rent, and you can be assured that you have complied with the current regulations which will help to reduce any problems further down the line.
You can now start the entire process again or sit back and relax right?

Ok so not quite, I could end the book here, and you'd perhaps feel satisfied, but there is one last thing to discuss. This may be where most landlords think the work is done, admittedly they know there will be repairs further down the line but what most fail to do is place the final piece of the jigsaw.

Section 3 - letting and managing the property
The final chapter, keeping your tenants.

This may be one of the shortest chapters within the book, but it carries just as much weight as some of the longest ones. Every landlord knows that they will have to carry out minor repairs from time to time, along with the eventual and inevitable major upgrades or more frequent general carpet replacements. How the landlord deals with the smaller problems such as leaks, boiler breakdowns, electrical issues, damp problems, fence or roof repairs, tree maintenance or sticking doors will all reflect the tenant's longevity.

It is essential to change your mindset on such problems; it is an inevitable consequence of being a landlord that these smaller repairs will rear their ugly head over the course of a tenancy. If you view them as an inconvenience or a drain on your profitable funds then your actions, timeframe and quality of tradesman will all be reflected by this.

If you have a good, reliable, well-communicating tenant who not only pays in full and on time but looks after your property well, you need to keep hold of them, and at all costs, after all, it is far easier to keep a good tenant happy then to find another one just like them.

If you simply view these minor or even sometimes major issues as simple running costs of the business, then you can act swiftly and thoroughly which will reflect in your tenant's overall opinion of you. It really is just the same for tenants as it is landlords, they will not want to move and risk having their new landlord be the kind of person who makes them wait for repairs or intrudes on their personal space regularly and increases the rent unreasonably yearly.

Every time a medium to long-term tenant moves out from one of our properties, I would estimate that the total costs to restore the property to a good rentable standard would be somewhere in the region of £1000-£2000. This is generally a few new carpets, painting, general unreported repairs and clearances.

If a tenant moves out because the issues that they reported to you have not been addressed, then they will still be there waiting for you when they have left, along with many other minor repairs that they felt they could live with.

These repairs will still need to be carried out regardless, but now you have the added pressure of starting the tenant find all over again. You now have the costs and inconvenience of advertising the property, as well as the £1,000-£2,000 clean-up cost that could have been avoided, had they still been at the property.

We also have the council tax liability and the mortgage payments to cover while the property is empty. Transferring the gas, electric and water back into your name for liability purposes is a timely and frustrating experience.

All these are laborious, time-consuming, unnecessary tasks and carry further costs, all because you didn't fix that faulty shower, leaking tap or fuse that kept tripping.

This may be inconvenient somewhat for you, but the tenant lives at the property, has a shower every day or sees that leaking tap daily, and their frustrations quite rightly quickly mount but can be just as easily appeased.

You are able to change your mindset on the larger issues that arise also if you train yourself in the art of auto-suggestion.

For example, let's say the boiler is on its last legs, well if you followed the advice in this book you will have had an idea of its age before you bought the property in the first place. There is an argument here that you knew it was going to go so you should have worked that into either your negotiation or at the very least your costings.

Let's assume however that it isn't the oldest boiler in the world; you knew it was an older model from your research, but you didn't think it was going to fail so soon into the tenancy.

Ok, so you can view this as a major hassle, unforeseen expense and then procrastinate in getting it replaced as the cost is unexpected and higher than you would have thought.

You can risk upsetting the tenant as they have either a faulty, temperamental or worse, a broken boiler which leads them to move out and you are still lumbered with the inevitable cost of replacement. Or, you can look at it another way.

Most boilers come with a 7-10 year warranty these days, if you install a new boiler now then you are guaranteed peace of mind that the boiler will not cost you another penny for the next 7-10 years at the very least.

You get to keep your perfect tenant happy, and they hold you in such high regard for acting so efficiently, not so dissimilar to that of your new boiler.

This is how I look at every single repair now, I look at them as inevitable, so after they are repaired or replaced it is one less thing to worry about, this keeps the tenant happy, and a happy tenant is one that pays but more importantly one that stays.

Everyone is a winner in this scenario.

Remember right at the beginning of this book when I gave you the Robert G Allen quote that said, 'the future you see is the future you'll get'. Well ask yourself this question what future do you see? Visualise it, believe in it, and you will categorically achieve it.

I have been asked by many people on many occasions over many years now, how I have been so successful in the industry in a relatively short timeframe, given that I started out without any financial backing or real capital to invest. I never really knew how to answer this question previously, and for many years I often gave different and very vague or muddled answers until I read a book on the history of science that gave me some insight to this question. The quote in the book summed me up in one quick sentence, now when somebody asks me how I have been so successful in this industry I tell them this.

'When Sir Isaac Newton was asked how he discovered the laws of gravity he simply replied' "by thinking about it all the time."

I would, once again like to thank you from the very bottom of my heart for taking the time to read or listen to this book. I aim to help people as much as I can to obtain the kind of wealth and freedom that I have been able to achieve in such a relatively short time within this wonderful industry. if you have any feedback at all, please do get in touch with me. If you just want to chat then, please let me know, and I can arrange this for you or If you are interested in attending one of our training courses then please again get in contact with me. As a thank you for purchasing this book I will be able to arrange a discount, just mention this in your email, and I shall gladly oblige. You can contact us through our website at www.wiseowlproperty.co.uk or at davis@wiseowlproperty.co.uk

As well as thanking each and every one of you from the very bottom of my heart, my thanks go out to my family for allowing me the time to write this book. Especially my wife who has been so understanding and time giving, raising our newborn, or not so newborn as they are now, twins along with our other two ever demanding children.

I would like to extend a special & personal thank you to my dad who from an early age has taught me the value of service or more accurately the rewards of doing a job right. It gave me the tools needed to progress beyond most others and without his initial lessons on the value of money, I am not sure where I would be at this time in my life.

I'd like to ask each of you for one small favour, if you have enjoyed this book, found it helpful then please take 2 minutes to write me a short review on Amazon. It would mean a great deal to me to read your positive comments.

Thanks and good luck on your journey.

www.wiseowlpropertytraining.co.uk/

My top reads in no particular order:

- Rich Dad Poor Dad – Robert Kiyosaki
- Financial I.Q Robert Kiyosaki
- The Richest Man in Babylon – George S. Clason
- The Gratitude Effect – Dr John Demartini
- The Laws of Success – Napoleon Hill
- The E Myth – Michael E. Gerber
- Ego is the Enemy – Ryan Holiday